Key Things Parents Should Know about Education *in* Indiana

Key Things Parents Should Know about Education *in* Indiana

Greater Educational Opportunities Foundation
Parent Information and Resource Center
Indianapolis, IN

Published by Greater Educational Opportunities Foundation
302 S. Meridian St. #201
Indianapolis, IN 46255

Publisher's Cataloging-in-Publication Data
Key things parents should know about education in Indiana : [empowering parents with information / Greater Educational Opportunities Foundation Parent Information & Resource Center ; edited by Joyce Johnson]. —Indianapolis : Greater Educational Opportunities Foundation Parent Information & Resource Center, 2005.

p. ; cm.
ISBN: 0-9765067-0-X

1. Education—Parent participation—Indiana. 2. School choice—Indiana. I. Title. II. Greater Educational Opportunities Foundation (Indianapolis, Ind). Parent Information & Resource Center. III. Johnson, Joyce.

LC225.32.I6 K49 2005
379.1/1—dc22 2005-921482

Book production and coordination by Jenkins Group, Inc.
www.bookpublishing.com
Interior design by Debbie Sidman
Cover design by Kelli Leader

Printed in the United States of America
09 08 07 06 05 • 5 4 3 2 1

GEO Mission

The Greater Educational Opportunities Foundation
believes that all children deserve access to a quality education.
We embrace all quality educational options that enable parents
to help their children learn and schools succeed.
Through our community outreach, educational awareness programs,
promotion of options that empower families, and creation of new options,
GEO strives to make educational choice a reality for all families.

Kevin Teasley
GEO Founder and President

Joyce Johnson
GEO Vice-President of Advancement
Executive Director, Parent Information and Resource Center (PIRC)
Editor, *Key Things Parents Should Know about Education in Indiana*

Keri Hunter
Director, Educational Leadership, PIRC

Tishika Jackson
Director, Parent Leadership, PIRC

The GEO Foundation is recognized by the IRS as a 501(c)3 nonprofit organization. GEO's taxpayer ID number is 95-4406881. Contributions to GEO are tax deductible.

ABOUT THE GEO FOUNDATION

The Indianapolis-based **Greater Educational Opportunities Foundation** (GEO), a leader in the effort to help disadvantaged families gain more educational options for their children, has established a **GEO-Parent Information and Resource Center** (GEO-PIRC) with innovative and research-based strategies to build the capacity of public school parents to participate as effective stakeholders in their children's education, as prescribed by No Child Left Behind (NCLB).

The **GEO Foundation** was founded in 1998 upon the belief that all children should have equal access to a quality education. Through community outreach, educational awareness programs, promotion of options that empower families, and creation of new options, GEO strives to make a quality education a reality for *all* families.

In Indiana, GEO's efforts helped pave the way for a charter school law, which was passed in 2001. GEO organized community leaders and opened the 21st Century Charter School in the fall of 2002, authorized by Indianapolis Mayor Bart Peterson. Sponsorship of this charter school has positioned GEO to understand parent concerns, the current educational bureaucracy, and the challenges associated with NCLB outreach and implementation.

GEO's staff, comprised primarily of parents, is uniquely qualified in the education arena with proven ability to implement a vision, extensive experience and knowledge of education reform issues, a national network of supporters, and more than 40 years of combined experience working directly with families for parental empowerment policies in K-12 education.

No *Parent* Left Behind

Throughout Indiana, there are thousands of parents whose children are attending failing schools. Although most of these parents are from disadvantaged, low-income, minority, and limited-English-proficient neighborhoods, they are willing to address the issues that keep their children from succeeding at school. They just don't have the information, confidence, or skills to make it happen.

GEO-PIRC provides "Parents as Leaders" training to equip parents to effectively evaluate data related to school educational performance standards. This training helps parents understand state proficiency test scores, educational options, and the rights and responsibilities available under NCLB, including public school choice and supplemental educational services. "Parents as Leaders" training enables parents to organize and become a dynamic force for school improvement and academic achievement for *all* children.

In addition, GEO has developed an aggressive media campaign using radio spots, billboards, signs on busses, and direct mail to create community demand for the improvement of low-performing schools and implementation of NCLB. Through this media outreach, GEO is providing hope and encouraging action.

Contents

Foreword

The United States Department of Education is pleased to support the work of the GEO Foundation through a grant to create *Key Things Parents Should Know about Education in Indiana*. This book is a resource that parents and families can use to learn about their educational options at every age and stage of life. This book covers a wide array of topics, from early childhood education and preparing children for success in school, to the options families have within the education system, to college and vocational information, to adult education, along with other topics important to Hoosier families, such as emergency services, housing and nutrition. The US Department of Education's Office of Innovation and Improvement recognizes GEO's work in supporting the goals of No Child Left Behind and ensuring that parents have the information they need to make the best educational choice for their families

Nina S. Rees
Assistant Deputy Secretary
Office of Innovation and Improvement
U.S. Department of Education

Acknowledgments

Writing a book is always a collaborative effort.
Key Things Parents Should Know about Education in Indiana is the work of many talented and committed writers and researchers.
The GEO Foundation wishes to acknowledge and thank:

Angi Parker Johnson, primary writer and researcher;
Connie Pulliam, creator and inspiration for the first GEO publication, *The GEO Educational Resource Guide*;
Cynthia Proffitt, contributing content, editing, and proofreading;
GEO-PIRC Parent Advisory Council, reviewing and making invaluable suggestions; and
GEO Staff for editing and proofreading.

We are also grateful to **USA Funds**
and the **U.S. Department of Education, Office of Innovation and Improvement, Parental Options and Information,**
for generous grants that made the publication possible.

USA Funds® is the nation's leading education loan guarantor and the designated guarantor of federal education loans in Indiana. A nonprofit corporation, USA Funds enhances postsecondary education preparedness, access, and success by providing and supporting financial and other valued services. During the past 44 years, USA Funds has supported more than $115 billion in financial aid for higher education and served more than 13.6 million students and parents, as well as thousands of educational and financial institutions. For more information, visit http://www.usafunds.org on the Web.

Key Things Parents Should Know about Education in Indiana
is a publication of the GEO Foundation
Parent Information and Resource Center.

Introduction

Dear Parents:

You are the single biggest influence on your children's education. Of course, you know that. But sometimes, it is difficult to know what school to choose or what tutoring programs are available, let alone your rights and opportunities.

That's why I am happy the Greater Educational Opportunities Foundation's (GEO) Parent Information and Resource Center has published ***Key Things Parents Should Know about Education in Indiana***. Page by page, this wonderful source of information seeks to help parents identify a variety of issues and topics that will aid in turning them into the educational leaders their children need so they may become successful scholars.

At GEO, we have designed several programs to empower parents with information required to participate as effective stakeholders in their children's education; whether it's helping them understand test scores or their rights under the No Child Left Behind Act through training and seminars, ***Key Things Parents Should Know about Education in Indiana*** is yet one more way of accomplishing our parent empowerment goals.

Remember, we all have a stake in the education of our children, not just with our own but also with those around us, so I encourage you to pass ***Key Things Parents Should Know about Education in Indiana*** on to someone you know who could benefit from reading it as well.

I hope you find the information contained within these pages all you need to help you shape your child so that he or she will have the ability to make that impact. I also hope to hear from you if you have information about additional programs we should include in future guides.

As always, GEO continues to be happy to serve the parents of tomorrow's leaders.

Sincerely,

Kevin Teasley
Founder and President
Greater Educational Opportunities Foundation (GEO)

An Invitation

Dear Parents,

At the Greater Educational Opportunities Foundation (GEO), we have faith in parents. We recognize that parents are their children's first and best teachers, and we believe that the more we can help parents understand what is expected of them, of their students, and of their schools, the greater the chances are that parents will get involved and become a dynamic force for education reform for all children.

Today, the Internet has made it possible to find an amazing amount of data about almost any topic, including education. However, most parents are busy trying to keep up with the pace of day-to-day living, and many don't have time to do all the research on education that they would like to do. They read the papers or listen to the news, and they know that the Indiana Department of Education releases an annual list of schools "in need of improvement." They know that there is an educational crisis in many communities in Indiana, such as Gary or Indianapolis, where many of the schools are performing poorly. But many parents wonder, What does that really mean for *my* child? Is this something that I should be concerned about? Is there something I can do? Is there something I *should* do?

One of the goals of the GEO Foundation's Parent Information and Resource Center (GEO-PIRC) is to develop resources and information that enable parents to make the best educational choices for their children. *Key Things Parents Should Know about Education in Indiana* is one of those tools, and it contains a wealth of information that covers every aspect of a child's educational adventure, from finding good-quality child care to preparing for college. We hope that you will find it helpful, use it often, and share it with others. Your feedback is welcome, and we'd love to hear how you have applied the information to make choices for your family or to work with your school.

GEO has a number of programs to assist parents with educational issues. We offer training for parents to understand Indiana school accountability, academic standards, and the opportunities for supplemental educational services and public school choice under the No Child Left Behind Act (NCLB). We focus on low-performing schools, and we strive to enhance academic achievement through parent empowerment. We publish a quarterly newsletter and offer workshops. We believe that NCLB offers new opportunities for parents and students and empowers *all* parents to be involved in a meaningful way in the process of school improvement for *all* children.

Each of us at GEO has dedicated our lives to the pursuit of a quality education for all children. Our GEO team is comprised of executives, moms, dads, educators, grandmothers, and college students, all with years of experience in the education arena. It is gratifying work. There is no greater cause than the future of our children, and **we invite you to be a part of our team.** Here are just a few of the ways you can get involved:

- **Read our newsletter.** *GEO for Families* will keep you informed of new educational choices and opportunities. If you don't receive it, just call our office at (317) 524-3770 and ask to be placed on the *GEO for Families* mailing list. **It's absolutely free!**
- **Let us hear *your* story.** If you are in need of more educational choices for *your* child, let us know. We may be able to help.
- **Attend GEO-sponsored educational forums and seminars** to learn more about current educational issues. We have several of these events each year, and most of them are free.
- **Attend your local school board meetings** and take a friend. (Make it a night out.) Voice your opinion and concerns. To find out when the board meets, call *your* local school or check their Web site.
- **Write a letter to your elected officials.** This is one of the most effective tools for letting your voice be heard. It is important for your representatives to know that you want quality educational choices, and each letter makes a big difference. If you are unsure about the process, give us a call; we'd be glad to help.
- **Write a letter to the editor of your local newspaper.** *Your* voice and concerns cannot be heard if you don't speak out. We have a staff with journalism experience, and we can help you get your story or opinion printed.

We invite you to give us a call today! We are enthusiastically looking forward to having you join with us in an effort to improve academic performance and increase educational options for all students in Indiana.

Sincerely,

Joyce Johnson
Executive Director, GEO Parent Information and Resource Center
Editor, *Key Things Parents Should Know about Education in Indiana*
September 2004

Editor's note: Web sites and contact information in this publication are presented only as suggestions of resources available. *Inclusion should not be considered an endorsement, and parental discretion is recommended.* Information presented was accurate at the time of publication. We regret any subsequent changes that may cause any inconvenience. Contact us at the GEO Foundation for further information.

PART I

Keys to Parent Involvement and School Choice

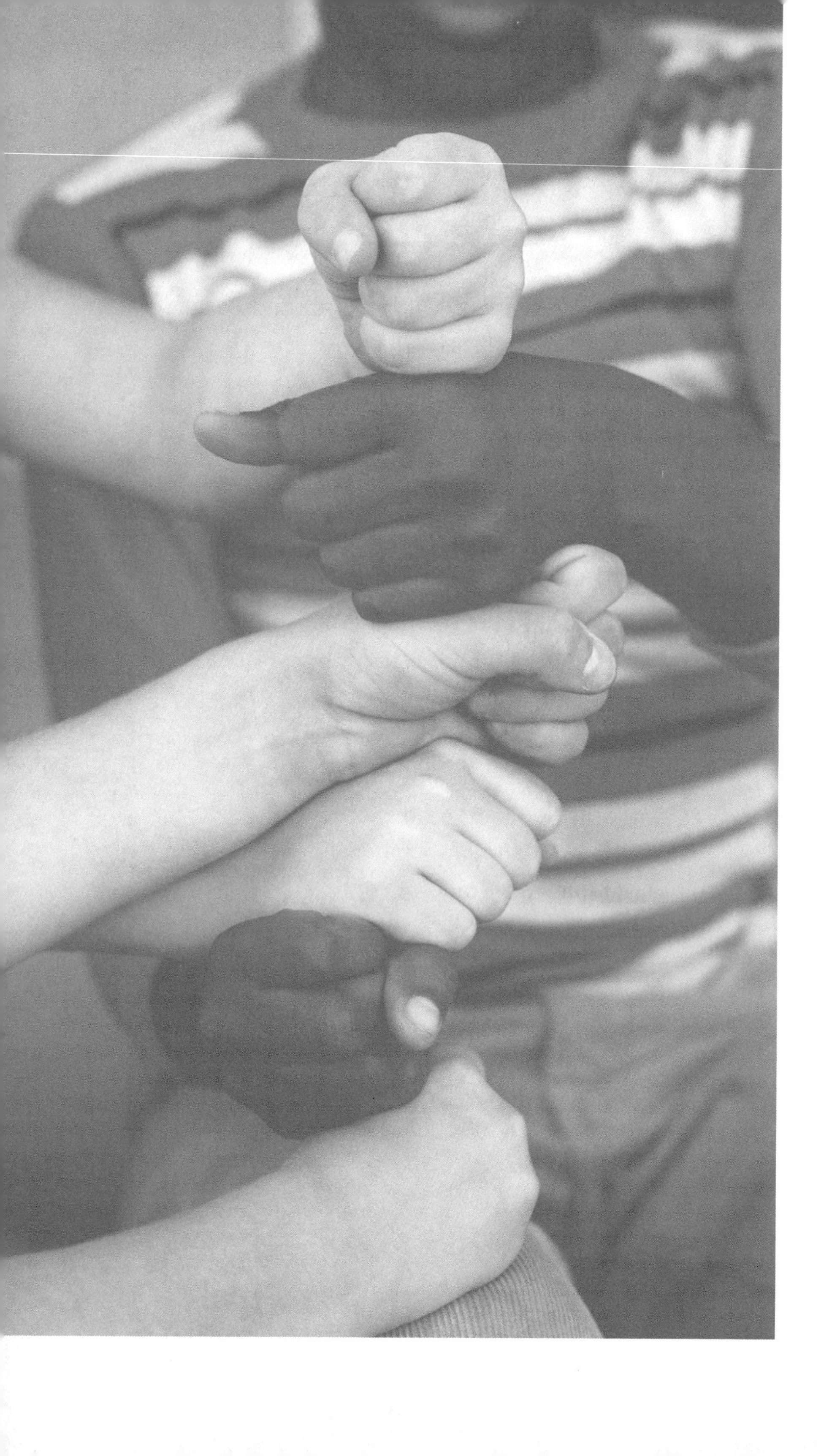

PARENTAL INVOLVEMENT

At GEO, we are convinced that the most important factor leading to a child's success in school—success that extends beyond academics—is an involved parent.[1] Children who have involved parents have greater academic success, such as better grades, but they also attend school more frequently, display appropriate behavior at school, have better social skills, and are more likely to go to college. Research shows that **schools also benefit from parent involvement.**

A review of dozens of studies of parent involvement has led researchers to the conclusion that **parent involvement in children's learning is positively related to achievement.** The studies convincingly show that parental involvement supports students' learning, behavior, and attitudes regardless of factors such as parents' income, educational level, and whether parents are employed.

However, the typical definition of parental involvement in most schools today is passive, with parents relegated to organizing bake sales and chaperoning field trips. Research has shown that when schools are open to parent and community participation in decision making, teachers implement more innovative practices and students do better academically—at least at the elementary level.[2]

Research on parent/community groups organized for school improvement is in its infancy. Such groups, specifically targeting academic achievement, have been in existence less than a decade, but the evidence is clear: *when parents have a sense of confidence and power, their children do better in school.*[3]

Parents have a powerful role to play to ensure that their children receive a quality education. A priority of the GEO-PIRC is to impact the performance of students and increase academic achievement by increasing parental investment in the educational process.

What Is Parental Involvement?

Being an involved parent can mean a lot of different things. Parents can be as involved as they wish to be on the basis of their availability and interest. Involvement can be as simple as checking a child's homework regularly or as much as running for school board!

---

[1]Throughout this resource guide, the term "parent" refers to the primary individual or individuals responsible for raising and caring for a student.

[2]Byrk, S., Easton, J.Q., Kerbow, D., Rollow, S., and Bender Sebring, P. *Charting Chicago School Reform: Democratic Localism as a Lever for Change.* Boulder, CO: Westview Press, 1998.

[3]If you are interested in additional information on research studies demonstrating the importance of parental involvement, see *A New Wave of Evidence: The Impact of School, Family and Community Connections on Student Achievement*, by Karen Mapp and Anne Henderson. This publication can be downloaded in its entirety from the Southeast Educational Developmental Laboratory Web site, http://www.sedl.org/connections/resources/evidence.pdf.

Here are some examples of ways parents can be involved with their child's education:

- Take your child to school on the first day of school.
- Make sure your child is prepared for each school day by eating a nutritious breakfast, wearing weather-appropriate clothes, and being well rested.
- Get all required school supplies the first week of school or sooner.
- Let your child know that school is important. Ask questions about school and homework *every* day and LISTEN! Set up a quiet place to do homework.
- Read *everything* that is sent home from the school such as report cards, homework assignments, school lunch plans, and vacation and bus schedules. This shows your child that parents are interested and well informed.
- Learn and talk about with your child the life skills being taught at school (e.g., respect, honesty, listening, etc.).
- Get to know your child's teacher and school principal by attending school meetings and parent/teacher conferences.
- Ask for copies of school policies (e.g., attendance, discipline). Ask lots of questions!
- Volunteer to help with school activities or attend field trips and fundraisers, or volunteer in the classroom or office.
- Offer to speak in the classroom about your hobbies, job, or career.
- Visit your child's classroom while school is in session! Some schools prefer that you set this up in advance with the school office and teacher.
- Talk to other parents. If there is a parent organization, such as the PTA or PTO, join it! If not, start one! Two or three interested parents are enough to start a group.
- Encourage your child to read at home. Visit the library and bookstore often with your child and read *with him or her*.
- Vote in school board elections.
- Limit the amount of time your child spends with television and video games on school nights.

CHOOSING THE RIGHT SCHOOL

Parents are the leading experts on what is best for their own children. They love their children and want what is best for them in all areas of life, including their education. Finding the right school is important, and there are choices!

In Indiana, families have several educational choices: public schools, magnet schools, charter schools, private or parochial schools, and home schooling. Each of these choices is discussed in detail on the following pages, and there are pros and cons for each choice. You are encouraged to consider the characteristics of quality schools described on the following pages when considering each choice because each choice may be a "quality choice" for your child.

There are many things to consider when choosing where and how your child is to be educated. Every child is unique with individual strengths and challenges, and some children require a nontraditional approach to learning. The more you know about the educational options available, the easier it is to find the right learning environment for your child.

Listed below are some things to consider when making this important decision for your child and your family:

- Available schools within the geographic area
- Availability of transportation
- Expense (tuition, etc.)
- Availability of financial aid and/or scholarships
- Faith-based affiliation
- Your child's strengths and challenges
- Your child's unique learning style or preference
- Safety and environment

Once the choices have been narrowed down, the next step is to do some basic research. The following suggestions will help you make an informed school choice:

1. **Begin by gathering information.**
   - Recommendations from friends, family, neighbors, or faith-based organizations and community leaders are a good place to start.
   - Call the schools for brochures or admission information.
   - Review Web sites that provide general information about public, private, and charter schools, such as http://www.greatschools.net.

2. **Visit the schools.**
   - Visiting schools provides an opportunity to learn about things that don't show up on reports.

- Make an appointment to see the school *without* your child. Teachers and school administrators should appreciate your concern and welcome your visit.
- Plan *in advance* what you will look for in the school and what type of questions you are going to ask, such as those about curriculum and compliance with state standards.
- On a separate visit, take your child to visit the school. Your child should be comfortable with the school, too.

3. **While at the school, you can learn a lot by noticing:**
   - Are the buildings maintained well?
   - Does the school feel like a safe place for children?
   - How do administrators and teachers greet you?
   - What do the school administrators and teachers talk about? How do they talk about the school?
   - Do children treat each other and teachers with respect?
   - What kind of equipment and resources does the school have?
   - What is the approximate class size?
   - Is there a level of diversity in the school and among the staff?
   - Are there bulletin boards and/or attractive displays with age- and grade-appropriate work?
   - What are the classrooms like? Are they quiet or chaotic?
   - Do students have access to computers and modern technology?
   - Is computer technology appropriately used and monitored in the classroom?

4. **Be prepared to ask questions of the principal and teachers** to learn what is most important to you and your child. You might ask:
   - What is the educational philosophy? (for example, lecture, large/small groupings, team teaching)
   - What life skills are taught and demonstrated in the school?
   - What are the academic standards? Do the standards conform to Indiana's standards of educational proficiency? How are they measured?
   - What percentage of students passes Indiana proficiency tests?
   - Is the school making "adequate yearly progress" (AYP), or is it "in need of improvement"?
   - How are students graded? How are these grades reported to parents?
   - Are teaching styles adaptable to student needs?
   - How do teachers and the school help when a student is having difficulty in a subject or behavior?
   - How are classes and teachers assigned? Are there teachers' aides?

- Are all of the teachers "highly qualified" and teaching in their area of expertise?
- What ongoing teacher training is available to teachers? Is it mandatory or optional?
- Are other professional specialists available, such as speech therapists, librarians, social workers, counselors, and psychologists?
- What are the school policies, such as attendance and discipline? How are policies enforced?
- How often are textbooks and class materials reviewed and updated?
- What process does the school use for self-evaluation? How are the results incorporated into the curriculum or policy?
- What transportation options are available?
- What extracurricular activities does the school offer?
- Is there a dress code or uniform policy?
- How are parents involved in the school?
- Are teachers, principals, and other staff members available to meet with parents during and after school hours? Can teachers be contacted by telephone or e-mail?
- Does the school have a Web site, homework hotline, or other resources to aid in student/teacher/parent information sharing?

5. **If you are visiting a private school**, you will want to ask about tuition costs and the availability of financial aid and/or scholarships. If the school is faith based, you may also want to ask:
   - How are faith and values incorporated into the education?
   - Must you belong to the congregation to attend? Is there a difference in tuition if you do not belong to the congregation?
   - What religion classes are taught? Are they mandatory?
   - What are the school's faith expectations of children who attend?
   - What is the dress code or uniform policy?

Be assured that as a parent, it is both your right and responsibility to make decisions regarding your child's education. The questions above may or may not cover the issues that most interest you and your child. You should feel free to ask about what matters to you.

And remember, because *you are the expert regarding your child*, you have a right to be treated as the expert. Your opinions should be respected, and you should have access to any information that is pertinent and important to your child. Plan to invest time in making this important decision, and involve your child. You, your child, and the school will benefit from your caring and concern.

WHAT MAKES A QUALITY SCHOOL

Parents want quality schools, and children deserve quality schools. But what *is* a quality school? Although the answer may vary because of special family interests and priorities, there are some basic research-based criteria to look for when evaluating a child's current or potential school. Parents should remember that a quality school does not have to be attractive from the outside or be located in a "good neighborhood." *The qualities that really matter are inside the school,* ***not outside.***

A quality school has:

- Strong, professional administrators and teachers who treat students, parents, and all involved adults with respect.
- A broad, expanding curriculum that is available to all students.
- A belief that all children can learn if taught and the presence of high expectations for all students according to their ability.
- A school climate that is safe, clean, caring, and well organized.
- An ongoing evaluation of the school, teachers, and students that is easily accessible to parents.
- A high level of parent and community involvement.

Quality schools welcome parent/community involvement and are eager and willing to answer questions and allow parents and community members to be involved in all aspects of the school.

Let's look at each of these qualities more closely.

Administrator

Quality schools have a strong administrator (principal) who:

- Leads instruction at the school and has in-depth knowledge of the school's curriculum, learning standards, and instruction provided at each grade level.
- Helps teachers develop teaching strategies and techniques and encourages teamwork.
- Makes time for training teachers and all school staff.
- Knows about available community resources and informs parents when appropriate.
- Can be seen in and around the school.
- Knows the students (preferably by name) and has a positive relationship with them.
- Communicates regularly with parents and takes the time to talk with and meet with individual parents.
- Values diversity and maintains a well-balanced staff.

- Works to maintain a positive attitude among staff to reduce turnover.
- Keeps class sizes appropriate.
- Develops, *with the input of staff and parents*, clear policies on attendance, discipline, and standards.

Teachers

Quality schools have professional and invested teachers who:

- Hold up-to-date certifications in the subject(s) they are teaching.
- Expect and encourage students to do their best.
- Teach students how to learn.
- Are willing to adapt teaching styles to meet students' needs.
- Provide students with lots of opportunities to practice new skills.
- Hold students responsible for completing assigned work correctly and on time.
- Set challenging and interesting assignments that relate to lessons.
- Respect diversity and relate lessons, as much as possible, to students' backgrounds, communities, and cultures.
- Maintain control in the classroom.
- Let students know on a regular basis how they are doing and what they are doing next.
- Use tests to evaluate the students *and* their own teaching styles.

Curriculum

Curriculum, or the courses offered, is an important consideration when evaluating a child's current or future school. A quality school recognizes diversity in backgrounds, strengths, needs, and goals of schools and develops a curriculum that focuses on these things. A school's curriculum should be as diverse as its students because diversity provides an opportunity to develop critical thinking and problem-solving skills, accept differences, and break down prejudices and stereotypes.

At a quality school, the curriculum:

- Places a strong emphasis on basic subjects, including science, math, language, and history.
- Includes fine arts, such as music and art instruction.
- Fits within the state and local guidelines for learning standards.
- Values diversity and encourages students to experience other cultures.
- Has flexibility to improve by offering more courses in different subject areas.
- Is evaluated regularly, and changes are made as needed.
- Focuses efforts on improving social, as well as academic, skills and prepares students for college, the workforce, and success in everyday living.

High Expectations

In quality schools, high expectations for student performance can be seen throughout the school. School bulletin boards, classroom displays, and hallway decorations send the message that academic achievement is valued. The overall environment says that learning is important and is rewarded for all students.

A quality school:

- Promotes learning as the most important reason for attending school.
- Sets high standards for assignments and is consistent with these standards.
- Provides lessons that are challenging but appropriate for each student.
- Uses class time for learning with few interruptions.
- Assigns homework with a purpose and in reasonable amounts.
- Checks and reviews homework.
- Sets high standards for classroom behavior to create a quiet and safe environment for learning.
- Rewards students for various academic achievements (not just good grades) at public assemblies to make a statement that learning is important.
- Makes resources available to assist teachers and students in improving their learning.
- Believes all students can learn if properly taught and shows this by making sure that all students have qualified teachers and updated materials.

The Environment

Children often learn as much from other students as they do from their teacher. Quality schools recognize this and create an environment that is safe, clean, and well organized throughout the school, not just in the classroom.

A quality school:

- Develops a strong sense of school spirit. Students are proud of their school and feel like they belong and are wanted by the school.
- Offers appropriate supervision to keep students safe and where they need to be while on school grounds.
- Keeps buildings in good condition.
- Recognizes and responds properly to students who come from many different home environments.
- Makes every effort to help students feel that the school is understanding and helpful with challenges and difficulties.
- Has a library stocked with up-to-date books for each grade level and teaches students how to use the library.
- Keeps hallways clean and neat.

Persistently Dangerous Schools

In Indiana, a review panel of state and local safety experts may identify a school as "persistently dangerous" if the school meets the state criteria three years in a row. The criteria for "dangerous" schools involve monitoring student criminal convictions and delinquency involving violence or possession of weapons and associated with school property, the school day, or school functions. Too many students involved in these dangerous activities over a period of time may mean that the school is "persistently dangerous."[4]

A child attending a "persistently dangerous" school is eligible for the public school choice options under No Child Left Behind, as is any student who has been the victim of a violent crime on the grounds of his or her school. (See NCLB, page 92.)

School Performance

Quality schools are concerned not only with student achievement but also with the performance of the school itself. Quality schools evaluate performance regularly and are honest when evaluating students, learning standards, and the curriculum. Quality schools make an effort to improve when necessary.

A quality school:

- Establishes clear goals for learning.
- Informs parents of standards for students and the school.
- Keeps parents informed about how students and the school are performing.
- Involves parents in planning for improvements for students and the school.

Now that you have reviewed the characteristics of a quality school, you may find yourself wondering, "What can I do to make sure my child's school is a quality school?" The answer is to be involved! While all of the characteristics listed above are important, parental involvement is the most significant factor in student success. You do your part to create a quality school for your child by asking questions and being involved!

---

[4]"Indiana Policy under the Unsafe School Choice Option, No Child Left Behind Act of 2001," adopted April 30, 2003.

EDUCATIONAL CHOICES IN INDIANA

In Indiana, families have several educational choices. Each of these choices is discussed in detail on the following pages. Because there are pros and cons for each choice, parents are encouraged to consider what makes a quality school when considering each choice. Each option could be a "quality choice" for a child.

- **Public Schools:** Government funded and operated.
- **Magnet Schools:** Government-funded public schools with specialized curriculum and facilities.
- **Charter Schools:** Government funded but privately operated.
- **Private Schools:** Privately operated and funded; may be faith based or secular.
- **Parochial Schools:** Private schools funded and administered by faith-based organizations.
- **Home Schooling:** Privately funded, under the direction of parents.

Public School Education

Public education is the choice of most parents in Indiana and throughout the United States. Public schools are funded by federal, state, and local taxes and are governed by local school board members elected by the community. In Indiana, 1,010,688 students were enrolled in 1,843 public schools during the 2003–2004 school year.

In 2004, 24 percent of the public schools in Indiana did not make "adequate yearly progress." There are efforts taking place on local, state, and federal levels to improve these schools. Information about local initiatives can be obtained from your child's school district and school.[5]

The most significant federal initiative is the No Child Left Behind Act, signed by President Bush in 2001. You can find out more information about this act at the official government Web site, http://www.nclb.gov. The law provides opportunities for families of students enrolled in schools that are "in need of improvement," including choosing a higher-performing public school or free tutoring.

It should be noted that there is uniformity among public school systems with regard to state standards and expectations, but some districts are well funded and offer great facilities, while other districts are financially strapped and offer students much less. Indiana schools have not yet achieved equality in the educational system.

---

[5]Indiana Schools up to Challenge; 76 percent Make Adequate Yearly Progress." Indiana Department of Education. http://www.doe.state.in.us/reed/newsr04/July2004/ayp2003table-release.html.

Indiana Department of Education (IDOE)
The IDOE Web site is a source of helpful information. The IDOE provides a "School Report Card" for each district and school, including a list of Indiana's 4-Star Schools, data on ISTEP+ test scores for each school, tutorial resources, and information about alternative education. More information can be found at http://www.doe.state.in.us or by calling, toll-free, (800) 833-2199.

http://www.greatschools.net
Another way to locate and evaluate schools in your area is to visit http://www.greatschools.net. On the Web site, select Indiana, and search by "address." The Web site allows visitors to review school profiles, compare schools in geographic areas, including charter and private schools, and track school performance, such as ISTEP+ scores and schools "in need of improvement."

http://imaps.indygov.org/schools/
For parents in the Indianapolis area, this Web site, sponsored by the Mayor's Office, includes a *Family Guide to Public Schools in Indianapolis*. This site has a very complete overview of schooling options in Marion County, including alternative public schools, magnet schools, and vocational schools.

Magnet School Education

By Steve Brockhouse, Assistant Director of Parental Options and Information, U.S. Department of Education, Office of Innovation and Improvement

Many school districts across the country use magnet schools to reduce minority group isolation; however, over time, the purposes of magnet schools have continued to evolve and expand. The U.S. Department of Education's federal Magnet Schools Assistance Program defines a magnet school as *a school that offers a special curriculum that is capable of attracting students of different racial backgrounds*. When the program was first authorized 20 years ago, its intent was twofold: to reduce, eliminate, or prevent minority group isolation in schools with substantial numbers of minority group students and to provide instruction in magnet schools that would substantially strengthen students' knowledge and skills. Since that time, expectations for magnet schools have grown to include enhancing student learning and narrowing the achievement gap, giving public school parents more choice in their child's education experience, and incubating innovative educational methods and practices that can raise the bar for all schools.

Specialties of magnet schools in Indiana include:

- Business and finance
- Communications arts
- Environmental studies

- Health professions
- Humanities
- Inquiry-based learning
- International studies
- Life science and wellness
- Math, science, and technology
- Multiple intelligences
- Montessori
- Performing and visual arts
- Telecommunications

Magnet schools are public schools and use different criteria and policies to select students for enrollment. Students wishing to attend a magnet school generally will be required to submit an application. In some instances, students are selected solely on the basis of their interest in attending a particular magnet school or program, and a lottery is used to determine which students will be selected if there are a greater number of applicants than a school has space to accommodate. Other schools may require that students meet established academic requirements or demonstrate particular skills or abilities through an audition, submission of a portfolio as part of their application, or writing an essay on a subject matter related to the magnet program.

Very few Indiana school corporations offer a magnet program at this time. Indianapolis Public Schools has a well-developed program, and information can be found at http://www.magnet.ips.k12.in.us/.

Charter School Education

Charter schools are innovative public schools providing choices for families and greater accountability for results. Chartering allows schools to run independently of the traditional public school system and to tailor their programs to community needs. While not every new school is extraordinarily innovative and some school operations may mirror those of traditional public schools, policy makers, parents, and educators are looking at chartering as a way to increase educational choice and innovation within the public school system.

Under Indiana code, charter schools are established to serve the different learning styles and needs of public school students, to offer public school students appropriate and innovative choices, to afford varied opportunities for professional educators, to allow freedom and flexibility in exchange for exceptional levels of accountability, and to provide parents, students, community members, and local entities with an expanded opportunity for involvement in the public school system. Like traditional public schools, charter public schools must have open enrollment policies and cannot discriminate based on disability, race, color, gender, national origin, religion, or ancestry.[6] There is no tuition at a charter school.

In 2001, the Indiana legislature was the thirty-eighth state to pass a charter school law. In the fall of 2004, 4,663 students were enrolled in 23 Indiana charter schools.[7]

Charter schools vary widely in educational philosophy and performance results. Parents should apply the same criteria for selecting a quality school regardless of the type of school. Additional questions parents should ask charter schools include:

- What are the grade configurations? Will my child be learning with children at his or her grade/age level?
- What extracurricular programs are available?
- How do students get to and from school?
- Is after-school programming available?
- How is my student's progress measured?
- When is my student eligible to move between grade levels?

Indiana Charter Schools

With the opening of the 2004–2005 school year, there will be 23 charter schools operating in Indiana on the elementary, middle, and high school levels. Charter school contact information is available from the Indiana Department of Education; the authorizers, the Mayor of Indianapolis and Ball State University; and the schools themselves.

If you are interested in learning more about charter schools, refer to one or more of the following Web sites:

Charter School Service Center	http://www.geofoundation.org
Indiana Charter Schools	http://www.doe.state.in.us/charterschools
Indiana Charter School Law and Resources	http://www.charterschoollaw.com
Authorizers:	
Mayor of Indianapolis	http://www.indygov.org/mayor/charter
Ball State University	http://www.bsu.edu/teachers/charter

[6]Indiana Charter School Law. Indiana Department of Education. November 7, 2004. http://www.doe.state.in.us/charterschools/welcome.html.

[7]"Charter Schools." Office of the Mayor, City of Indianapolis. http://www.indygov.org/eGov/Mayor/Education/Charter/home.htm.

Private and Parochial School Education

There are more than 800 privately operated (nonpublic) schools in Indiana. Private schools differ from public schools in funding and financial support. Because they do not receive government funding, they have the freedom to determine their own policies with regard to student enrollment, selection of curriculum and staff, etc.

Private schools are often created in support of a *mission* or *philosophy*. This statement usually provides a description of what the school believes is important. Some schools are religious or faith based ("parochial"); others might be focused on fine arts or science. Each school has a "flavor" of its own, offering a variety of services and/or programs that make it unique.

Private schools usually have tuition costs, some of which may seem very expensive. Before ruling out the private school option, take time to research financial aid opportunities. Many private schools offer need-based financial assistance and scholarships.[8] You can make an appointment with the school's admissions or financial director to discuss the options.

Locating Private Schools

Indiana Non-Public Education Association
1400 N. Meridian Street
Indianapolis, IN 46202-2367
(317) 236-7329
Fax: (317) 236-7328
http://www.inpea.org

The Indiana Non-Public Education Association (INPEA) is the largest state organization of private schools, representing more than 425 schools, 99,000 students, and 7,600 teachers, prekindergarten to twelfth grade.

These Web sites are useful in locating nonpublic schools in Indiana and throughout the nation. Most sites also provide direct contact information for each school.

American Association of Christian Schools, http://www.aacs.org
Association of Christian Schools International, http://www.acsi.org

---

[8]The **Starfish Initiative** assists promising disadvantaged students with an opportunity to attend private high school and provides mentoring to ensure that students graduate from high school and college. For more information, visit http://www.starfishinitiative.org, or call (317) 925-9415.

The **Educational CHOICE Trust** provides scholarship grants to students of lower-income families enabling them to attend private or parochial elementary schools of their choice. Scholarships are provided for up to one-half of the child's tuition, or $1,000 annually. The family is responsible for the remaining tuition. The Educational CHOICE Trust is a 501(c) (3) public charity funded by individual, corporate, and foundation contributions. Parents are encouraged to apply early in the spring for the following school year. For more information, visit http://www.choicetrust.org.

Boarding Schools, http://www.schools.com
This site provides nationwide information.
Catholic Schools, http://www.archindy.org
Elementary schools are listed by parish listings; high schools are listed individually.
Catholic Boarding Schools, http://www.cbsa.org
Christian Schools, http://www.christianschoolsusa.com
Independent Schools, http://www.isacs.org
Indiana Non-Public Education Association, http://www.inpea.org
Lutheran Schools, http://www.indylutheranschools.org
This site identifies Lutheran elementary and high schools in the Indianapolis area.
Montessori Schools, http://www.amshq.org
American Montessori Society provides lists of schools by state.
Private School Locator, http://www.nces.ed.gov
Seventh Day Adventist Schools, http://www.nadeducation.adventist.org

Home School Education

Home schooling is a growing choice for parents wishing to provide a personalized education for their children. Reliable estimates suggest that there are more than 50,000 children in Indiana being taught at home, and the number grows about 15 percent each year.[9]

Families give a variety of reasons for choosing to homeschool, including the home provides a safe environment in which to learn, free from drugs, violence, and negative peer pressures; students are able to progress at their own speed; curriculum can be individualized and can include strong basic education and special-interest studies; special needs or learning styles can be individually accommodated; instruction is one on one; family and/or faith-based values may be instilled.

It is legal to homeschool your children in Indiana. Home schools are considered to be private schools and are supported by the same state laws governing private schools. Parents do not need a special degree or credentials to teach their own children, and they do not need to be "certified." The requirement for state academic performance testing, such as the Indiana State Test of Educational Proficiency (ISTEP+), does not apply to home schools, although parents are encouraged to administer nationally normed tests.

On the positive side, home schooling offers parents great flexibility and control over the child's educational curriculum, life skills emphasis, and school policies, such as discipline and scheduling. On the other hand, a significant investment of time and resources is required of parents who choose

[9]The Indiana Department of Education (IDOE) has more than 25,000 families reporting, according to Lora Miller, IDOE Home School Liaison.

this educational option. In addition to planning, teaching, and documenting the curriculum, parents also need to meet their children's extracurricular need for activities such as the arts, physical fitness, and socialization opportunities. Home schooling requires a full-time effort to ensure your child has the learning tools he or she needs to succeed.

Additional Sources of Home School Information

For information on Indiana state law regarding home education, contact:

Lora Miller, Home School Consultant, Indiana Department of Education
(317) 232-9135
http://doe.state.in.us/sservices/hse.htm

Indiana Foundation for Home Schooling (IFHS)
P.O. Box 17385
Indianapolis, IN 46217
(317) 308-6411
http://www.IFHSonline.org

The IFHS is a good place to start for information about homeschooling. This organization has an excellent Web site with links to everything from getting started to high school graduation information. The IFHS also provides extensive information about African-American home schooling and other topics not typically covered in much detail on home school Web sites. The organization is also the sponsor of the Indiana statewide graduation ceremony and offers scholarships to college-bound home schooled students.

Indiana Association of Home Educators (IAHE)
8106 Madison Avenue
Indianapolis, IN 46227
(317) 859-1202
http://www.inhomeeducators.org

The IAHE, founded in 1983, has volunteer representatives throughout the state who are qualified to assist you in getting started. They can help answer questions, find resources, identify support groups, and suggest extracurricular learning experiences for your student. The IAHE sponsors an annual state convention each spring and provides a free bimonthly statewide magazine, *The IAHE Informer*, with valuable resources and tips for schooling your children.

"Homeschooling Your Children"
Barnes and Noble offers a free 24-hour, four-week online course that provides an overview of home schooling and its benefits and potential challenges. You can find more information at http://educate.barnesandnoble.com.

The **GEO Foundation** also has knowledgeable staff with years of home schooling experience who welcome an opportunity to talk about this option. For more information, call GEO at (317) 524-3770.

National Home School Organizations

Home School Legal Defense Association (HSLDA)
Box 3000
Purcellville, VA 20134
(540) 338-5600
http://www.hslda.org

This national organization advocates for families and home school freedom and provides legal protection for members.

National Black Home Educators Resource Association (NBHERA)
6943 Stoneview Avenue
Baker, LA 70714
nbhera@Internet8.net
Eric and Joyce Burges, Founders

National Home Education Network
http://www.nhen.org

The National Home Education Network encourages and facilitates the work of state and local home schooling organizations and individuals by providing information, fostering networking, and promoting public relations on a national level.

National Challenged Homeschoolers Associated Network (NATHHAN)
P.O. Box 39
Porthill, ID 83853
(208) 267-6246
http://www.nathhan.com

This national organization provides resources and a referral service for families and children with special needs.

FUTURE OPTIONS

Vouchers and Educational Tax Credits

Parental choice in education is a controversial issue. The most debated school choice options allow the use of public money to attend private and parochial schools, usually through a **voucher, tax credit, or tax deduction.** Some people believe that these options threaten the very existence of the public education system. Others believe that these options provide greater educational opportunities for students and, by introducing competition into the system, have the capacity to improve the performance of public schools. The GEO Foundation supports these educational options.

Definitions

- **Vouchers:** Parents are able to use money set aside for education by the state and federal government to send their child to the school of their choice. This could be a public, private, or faith-based school. **Indiana families do not yet have this option.**
- **Privately funded vouchers** are payments that a private organization makes to a parent, or an institution on a parent's behalf, to be used for a child's educational expenses. In Indiana, the **Educational Choice Charitable Trust** is an example of a private voucher program.[10]
- **Tax credits:** Tax credits can be a dollar-for-dollar refund for approved educational expenses such as books, supplies, computers, tutors, and, in some states, tuition and transportation. Programs vary from state to state with regard to the amount of credit families may claim. Also, in some states, tax credits are allowed before income tax is calculated; in other states, the taxes are reduced by the amount expended for educational materials, tuition, etc. In some states, tax credits may amount to $2,000 per family. **Indiana does not yet have this option.**

[10]The **CHOICE Trust** provides scholarship grants to students of lower-income families enabling them to attend private or parochial elementary schools of their choice. Scholarships are provided for up to one-half of the child's tuition, or $1,000 annually. The family is responsible for the remaining tuition. The Educational CHOICE Trust is a 501(c)(3) public charity funded by individual, corporate, and foundation contributions. Parents are encouraged to apply early in the spring for the following school year. For more information, visit http://www.choicetrust.org.

SCHOOL CHOICE FACTS

Compiled by the Alliance for School Choice, http://www.allianceforschoolchoice.org

- School voucher programs currently exist in Cleveland, Florida, Maine, Milwaukee, Vermont, and Washington, D.C. Florida also has a voucher program for disabled students.
- Scholarship tax credit programs exist in Arizona, Pennsylvania, and Florida.
- According to a recent Gallop poll on race and education, nearly four in 10 (38 percent) respondents believe that black children receive unequal educational opportunities.
- The average black high school senior graduates four grade levels below the average white high school senior.[11]
- Forty-four percent of black students and 46 percent of Hispanic students do not graduate from high school.[12]
- Twenty-seven percent of black high school dropouts ages 21–30 are currently in jail.[13]
- Hispanics are the most undereducated major segment of the U.S. population, according to the National Council of La Raza.
- While educational prospects for other minorities have improved during the past 20 years, several measures indicate that this is not the case for Hispanics.
- In some cities, as many as 85 percent of children from low-income families fail to graduate.[14]
- School choice programs have reduced the racial academic gap and boosted graduation rates.[15]
- School choice programs offer a competitive incentive that spurs public schools to perform better. Standardized test scores reveal that public schools competing with low-cost private schools score 2.7 national percentile points higher in eighth grade reading, 2.5 points higher in eighth grade math, 3.4 points higher in twelfth grade reading, and 3.7 points higher in twelfth grade math.[16]

---

[11]Thernstrom, A., and Thernstrom, S. *No Excuses.*

[12]Greene, J.P., Ph.D., and Forster, G., Ph.D. *Public High School Graduation and College Readiness Rates in the United States.*

[13]Neal, D. *Resources and Educational Outcomes among Black Children.*

[14]Bolick, C. *Voucher Wars.*

[15]Howell, W.G., and Peterson, P.E. *The Education Gap.*

[16]Minter Hoxby, C. Harvard University and Stanford University's Hoover Institute Study.

Parents afforded school choice for their children are more involved in their children's education and hold them and their schools to higher academic standards. By reasserting parental rights and the best interest of the child, school choice infuses accountability into the educational system and promotes educational opportunity where none previously existed.[17]

[17]Minter Hoxby, C. Center for Education Reform, Harvard University and Stanford University's Hoover Institute.

PART II

Key Educational Considerations

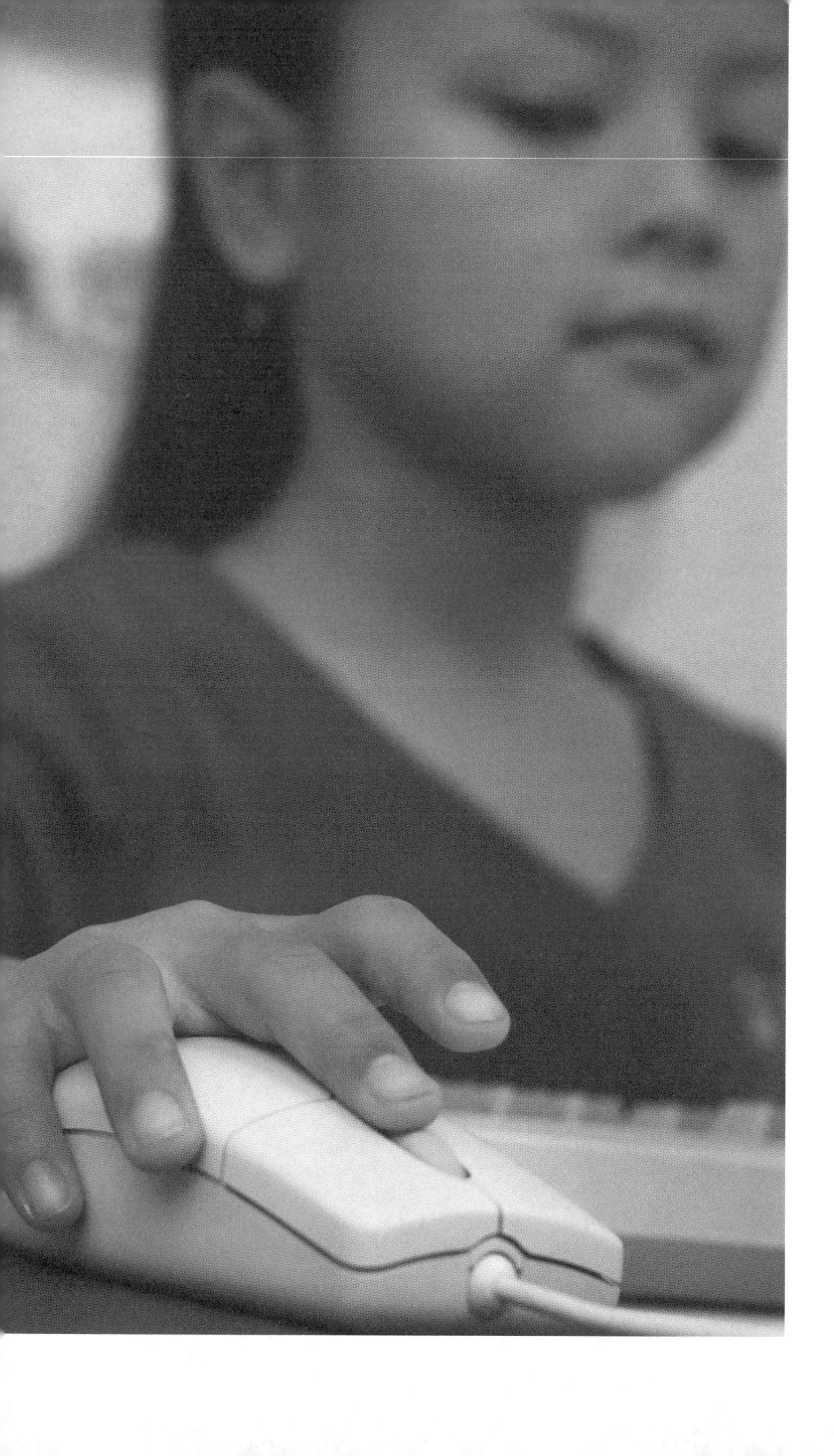

LITERACY

"If we can send a man to walk on the moon, surely we can teach every six-year-old in the United States to read."

—U.S. Deputy Secretary of Education Eugene W. Hickok, National Charter School Conference, Miami, Florida, January 2004

Of all the lasting gifts parents can give their children, one of the most important is that of ***literacy****—the ability to successfully read and comprehend what is read.* **Being able to read is the single most important predictor of academic success.** Parents can give their children a head start in life by teaching them to appreciate and understand the written word.

Today, large numbers of school children, including children from all social classes, face significant difficulties in learning to read. Schools are identifying an increasing number of students as "learning disabled"—a label most often associated with difficulty learning to read. Failure to learn to read is especially likely among poor children, members of a racial minority, or children whose native language is not English.

Historically, literacy skills were reserved for the scholars and religious leaders of society. The invention of the printing press, which made the written word available to all, and the changes that followed, has made literacy a universal right. At one time in our history, people were considered literate if they could just write their name. However, today's advanced society requires a level of literacy that includes not only reading and writing but also the ability to speak, listen, apply critical thinking skills, and access and use information effectively, with skills that foster lifelong learning or self-directed inquiry. To be employable in the modern world, you must be able to read challenging material.

It's Never Too Soon

The building blocks of literacy begin in the preschool years. Children who enter school with language skills and prereading skills—understanding that print reads from left to right and top to bottom—are more likely to learn to read well in the early grades and succeed in later years. In fact, research shows that most reading problems faced by adolescents and adults are the result of problems that could have been prevented through good instruction in their early childhood years.[18] It is never too early to start building language skills by talking with and reading to children. Children of all ages benefit from being read to by an adult.

---

[18]Snow, C.E., Burns, M.S., and Griffin, P. *Starting Out Right.* Committee on the Prevention of Reading Difficulties in Young Children, National Academy of Sciences, Washington, D.C., 1998.

**"You may have tangible wealth untold, caskets of jewels and coffers of gold.
Richer than I you can never be—I had a parent who read to me."**

—*Strickland Gillilan*

The section that follows includes information about how children get ready to learn to read and write. There are suggestions for what parents can do to foster literacy in children. There is also a valuable list of literacy and reading resources, materials, and community programs to encourage *all* children to learn how to read and how to enjoy it.

How Children Get Ready to Learn to Read and Write

What Parents Can Do to Help

Babies, from the time they are born, listen to the sounds adults make when talking, and as they get older, they try to imitate them. **Talk to your children—even when they are babies!**

At approximately 18 months old, babies understand common words and start to use them one by one. From there, babies learn to speak in two-word sentences and, eventually, more complex sentences. You can enhance a child's vocabulary by talking and reading to him or her. A child is NEVER too young to be introduced to language.

By preschool (ages 3 to 5), children can engage in complex conversations, story telling, expressing feelings, and even imitating adult writing. Preschool children start to notice printed words and recognize that they have meaning. They start to use visual cues to understand words. You can help by pointing out common words in books, on labels, and on signs. The foundation for learning to read and write is developing strong listening and speaking skills. You can lay that foundation by reading and talking to your children and encouraging them to ask questions. Children don't just suddenly learn to read. They build on years of informal and playful involvement with adults!

More Ways That Parents/Caregivers Can Help Children Become Successful Readers:

- **Teach your children to appreciate the written word.** Share stories with them and take every opportunity to point out ways in which reading is essential in everyday life—not just in school.
- **Read to your children from books** with easy-to-read large print. Help your children learn and recognize words that occur frequently (such as "a," "the," "is," "was," "you," etc.).
- **Teach the alphabet.** Encourage children with activities that help them recognize letters visually. Play games that use letters. Help children write their names and "sign" their artwork and projects.

- **Use nursery rhymes and repetitive songs** with children at an early age.
- **Teach the relationship of sound and letters.** Start with the more common letters, and present each letter. Model its sound and have your children produce the sound themselves. There are 26 letters in the alphabet, and they combine to make 128 sounds. When children recognize these letters and sounds, they can read!
- **Teach your children to sound out words.** Start with short words, and help your children to sound out letters one by one.
- **Teach your children to spell words.** Start with simple words!
- **Read daily with your children** to help them develop comprehension and reflective reading skills.
- **Encourage your child's imagination and comprehension by asking questions about the stories you read.**

If you are interested in learning more about encouraging your child to read or if you want to purchase recommended books or materials, a wealth of literacy information can be found on the Internet. Here are a few helpful national Web sites:

The National Right to Read Foundation
http://www.nrrf.org
This is the official Web site of the National Right to Read Foundation, whose mission is to return to American schools reading instruction that has been scientifically proven to be successful. It provides resources and research to teach children how to read.

The National Right to Read Foundation
P.O. Box 685
Manassas Park, VA 20113
Indiana: Anita Holten
holten@peoplepc.com
(574) 247-0605

Reading Is Fundamental
http://www.rif.org
Reading Is Fundamental is the nation's largest nonprofit children's literacy organization. The Web site includes a special section for parents.

Reading Is Fundamental Inc.
1825 Connecticut Avenue, N.W.
Suite 400
Washington, DC 20009
Toll free: (877) RIF-READ or (202) 673-0020

Get Ready to Read
http://www.getreadytoread.org
Get Ready to Read is sponsored by the National Center for Learning Disabilities. The Web site includes tools and resources for parents, educators, and health care professionals to insure that all preschool children have the skills they need to read by the time they enter school.

National Center for Learning Disabilities
381 Park Avenue S. Suite 1401
New York, NY 10016
(212) 545-7510
Fax: (212) 545-9665
Toll-free: (888) 575-7373
E-mail: help@getreadytoread.org

Proactive Parent
http://www.proactiveparent.com
This site is designed for parents by parents. It includes literacy and reading resources for all ages and skill levels.

Indiana Literacy Foundation
http://www.indianaliteracy.org
Literacy HelpLine: (317) 639-6106 ext. 211
The mission of the **Indiana Literacy Foundation** (ILF) is to increase literacy levels among the people of Indiana. The ILF works with 300 volunteer literacy programs across the state to develop their capacity to offer quality services to their communities. The ILF operates a helpline that provides children and adults with referrals to tutors and local literacy programs. A list of programs by county is included on the Indiana Literacy Foundation Web site.

CHILD CARE

Research has demonstrated that there is a strong relationship between the quality of child care and its impact on the development of young children. Decisions regarding child care should be made with a great deal of consideration and thought. There are many child care options available depending upon a child's age, availability of family and friends, the family financial situation, and personal preferences.

Child Care Options

Care Provided by Relatives, Friends, and/or Neighbors
This option is the most informal of child care options because there is no state or local regulation. However, many parents are most comfortable with this option because the caregiver has a personal relationship with the child and parent and shares an interest in the child, which often results in an increased level of trust. Care provided by relatives, friends, and/or neighbors can also cost less than other options.

In-Home Caregivers
In-home caregivers are professional child care providers who care for children in the family's own home. They are often called "nannies." For more information regarding in-home nannies:

All-American Nanny Ltd.
2120 Staples Mill Road, Suite 107
Richmond, VA 23230
Toll free: (800) 3-NANNYS
(804) 342-4200
Fax: (804) 342-9300
E-mail: nanny@pinn.net

Nanny on the Net
http://www.nannyonthenet.com/
Nanny on the Net Online Program has a fully searchable database and detailed system to finding and hiring a nanny.

Family Child Care
Child care is provided in the caregiver's home. **Family child care homes must be licensed by the state of Indiana** if the caregiver uses his or her home in caring for more than five children who are:

- Not a child of the caregiver,
- Unattended by their parent/guardian, and
- Given care for compensation.

The license is granted by the Central Office of the Indiana Division of Family and Children and authorizes operation of home child care at a specific location for a specific duration, specifying the maximum number of children for whom the home services can be provided.

To qualify for a license, the caregiver must successfully complete the following:

- Criminal background check and sex offender registry check for all adults in the home.
- Home inspection completed by Indiana Division of Family and Children staff.
- Doctor's statement confirming that the caregiver is healthy and physically able to perform necessary duties.
- Training of staff must include CPR, first aid, and early development.
- Staff must be at least 18 years old with a high school diploma. If working with infants/toddlers, staff should be at least 21.

Licensed child care homes must comply with state regulations regarding child to staff ratio, as follows:

- **Children 0-24 months** **6 children to 1 staff**
  (At least 2 children must be 16 months and able to walk or the ratio is 4 children to 1 staff.)
- **Children 0-6 years** **10 children to 1 staff**
  (There may be no more than 3 children less than 16 months.)
- **Children 3 years and older** **12 children to 1 staff**

Child Care Centers

Group care is provided for children in a public facility. **All child care centers are required to be licensed. Licensing does NOT insure quality** but does set minimum standards regarding health, safety, and caregiver training. Child care centers must be inspected for license renewal at least once a year.

Things to Consider

Regardless of which child care option you choose, it is important to take time to visit the homes and/or centers before making a final decision. All child care homes and centers should be eager to have you visit and willing to answer any questions you may have regarding their facility. A child's best interest should be everyone's number one priority!

Some things to look for when visiting prospective day care centers and family day care homes:

- Child to staff ratio, which meets state guidelines (see above).
- Children supervised at all times.

- Dedicated, friendly caregivers who are trained in child development, early childhood education, and/or a related field. (Don't be afraid to ask this question. It's your right to know.)
- Center or home is licensed and regularly inspected.
- Written policy regarding the care of ill children.
- Limited or no TV viewing. (TV viewing, if any, should be educational.)
- Safe sleep and play environments. (Cots are required for children ages 2 to 5. Infants should have their own crib or port-a-crib that meets safety standards.)
- Clean toys in good condition with no sharp edges or loose parts.
- Diapering area separate from play area.
- Perishable food refrigerated.
- Healthy meals/snacks provided regularly with a menu available for review.
- Cleaning supplies and other toxic materials in locked cabinet.
- Easily accessible first aid kit and posted emergency numbers.
- Electrical outlets should be covered with protective caps.
- Security gates at the top/bottom of all staircases.
- Window guards on all windows except for designated fire exits.
- Smoke alarms and fire extinguishers that work.
- All outside play areas enclosed with soft surfaces under all equipment.
- Emergency evacuation plan posted with regular drills.

Many organizations have developed guidelines and checklists on choosing child care based on research, observation, and experiences in the field. If you are interested in learning more about child care options or are in need of referrals to licensed centers and/or homes, the following Web sites contain valuable information:

Child Care Aware
http://www.childcareaware.org
1319 F Street NW, Suite 810
Washington, DC 20004-1106
(800) 424-2246

Children's Foundation (CF)
http://www.childrensfoundation.net
725 15th Street NW, Suite 505
Washington, DC 20005-2109
(202) 347-3300
CF is a private, national, educational nonprofit organization that strives to improve the lives of children and those who care for them. CF publishes an excellent fact sheet entitled *A Guide for Parents Using or Seeking Home-Based Child Care.*

Child Care Finder
http://www.childcarefinder.in.gov
This Web site is maintained by the Indiana Division of Family and Children and provides a child care locator; information regarding child care policies, rules, and laws; and a parent's guide to choosing safe and healthy child care.

Indiana Association for Child Care Resource and Referral
http://www.iaccrr.org
IACCRR works with agencies at the local, state, and national levels to provide, coordinate, and advocate for a strong statewide system of child care. It also provides resources and referrals, resulting in safe, healthy, and responsive care for all children.

National Association for the Education of Young Children (NAEYC)
1509 16th Street NW
Washington, DC 20036
(800) 424-2460
(202) 232-8777
NAEYC is the nation's largest organization of early childhood educators and others dedicated to improving the quality of programs for children from birth through third grade. Founded in 1926, NAEYC has more than 100,000 members and a national network of nearly 450 local, state, and regional affiliates.

The Indiana affiliate is:
Indiana AEYC
P.O. Box 88474
Indianapolis, IN 46208-0474
Toll free: (800) 657-7577

PREKINDERGARTEN

Learning does not begin when a child starts school. Learning begins the moment a child is born, and in fact, the crucial learning period *ends* at age five, when most children begin school. So, what does this mean for parents? As discussed in the section on literacy, parents can help their children get a healthy academic start by talking to them, reading to them, and instilling in them the importance of reading and education. Four-year-olds, and sometimes three-year-olds, often have the option of **prekindergarten**, or **preschool** education in a formal classroom setting. Parents are encouraged to use the same kind of discerning judgment in selecting a prekindergarten program for their children. Characteristics of a quality program are described below.

Researchers have documented that there are benefits of participation in prekindergarten programs for children. **Kathleen Cotton** and **Nancy Faires Conklin**, in a paper reviewing the research in early childhood education,[19] found that there are documented long-term advantages to quality prekindergarten programs.

Some long-term academic benefits for children who attend a prekindergarten program include:

- They are less likely to be held back or placed in special education classes.
- They display a significant increase in IQ scores.
- They have a better attitude toward school.
- They score higher on both math and reading achievement tests through the sixth grade.
- They are more likely to achieve higher grades and graduate from high school or get a GED.

When compared with children who did not attend a prekindergarten program, children who attended a quality prekindergarten program have:

- Higher earnings.
- Higher levels of schooling.
- Higher rates of home ownership.
- Fewer arrests.
- Lower involvement with social services.

[19]Cotton and Conklin. *Research on Early Childhood Education*. School Improvement Research Series, Northwest Regional Educational Laboratory. http://www.nwrel.org/scpd/sirs/3/topsyn3.html. 12/29/04.

Characteristics of a Quality Prekindergarten Program

- Class size is small with a low teacher to child ratio
- Comprehensive services are available, including health, nutrition, and social services
- Teacher qualifications: all teachers should have at least an associate's degree in early childhood development and should attend ongoing training
- Parents are encouraged to be involved and observe the class
- Developmentally appropriate curricula and learning materials are used
- Secure, safe environment, where safety is a priority
- Belief that children are individuals with unique learning styles
- Physical environment is well-organized with age-appropriate and culturally relevant materials
- Children engage daily in direct, hands-on learning
- Children have access to various activities throughout the day
- Children have the opportunity to play outside every day
- Teachers work with individual children, small groups, and the whole group at different times throughout the day
- Classroom is decorated with children's original artwork
- Children work on projects but also have long periods of time to play
- Teachers read to and with the children
- Children learn letters and numbers in the context of their everyday experiences
- Children and parents look forward to school

The benefits of a quality prekindergarten program are both powerful and long lasting for children, parents, and the community as a whole. Prekindergarten programs have proven so beneficial that some states, such as Georgia and New York, have started programs that provide prekindergarten for all children, and other states seem to be moving in that direction.

Currently, in Indiana, prekindergarten programs exist in both the private and public sector. Many of the private schools listed in the previous section offer prekindergarten programs, but they do require tuition.

Head Start

Since 1965, the federal government has sponsored Head Start to provide a comprehensive program with activities that promote social, emotional, and cognitive development, as well as health services, for children in poverty. Head Start funding goes directly from the federal level to local organizations, including public schools and community-based organizations. Head Start is one of many programs that provide approximately $23 billion in federal and state funds for child care and preschool education. Indiana offers the Head Start Program **free of charge** to those who meet income requirements. Information regarding

Indiana's Head Start Program can be found at http://www.in.gov/fssa/children/headstart, or you can contact them at (317) 233-6837.

Finally, inquire at your local school and/or churches about what prekindergarten programs are available. The rewards will last a lifetime!

Parents as Teachers (PAT)

President Bush's No Child Left Behind Act puts a special emphasis on doing what works. The PAT curriculum, for birth to five years old, is based on current research in the areas of child development, and training is directed toward the essential components of school readiness. Training for parents is presented in the home in the five key areas that determine success in school: physical well being, motor development, language development, what a child understands, and a child's general knowledge.

In Indiana, PAT training is available in more than 50 communities, and soon every county will offer training through Healthy Families, administered by the Indiana Family and Social Services Administration (FSSA). PAT training is free. You can locate the PAT program in your area by visiting the PAT Web site, http://www.patnc.org, or by calling Parents as Teachers National Center, (866) PAT-4YOU, (866) 728-4968.

SCHOOL-AGE CHILDREN

"Our children ... deserve an education worthy of this great nation. Together we will make sure that every child learns and no child is left behind."

—President George W. Bush

At the heart of the No Child Left Behind Act of 2001 is a promise to raise standards for all children and to help *all* children meet those standards. The law recognizes that parents are their children's first and most important teachers and that for children to be successful in school, parents and families need to be actively involved in their children's learning. They need to become involved early and stay involved throughout the children's school career.

In support of President Bush's commitment to giving parents and teachers tools to help children succeed, the U.S. Department of Education has developed a number of publications featuring the latest research and most effective practices in subjects such as reading, homework, and staying drug free. These publications are available in hard copy or online at http://www.ed.gov or from the GEO Foundation. Each is provided at no cost. The research-based yet easy-to-understand information in these publications can help families and educators make good decisions about children's learning. Well-informed parents and teachers are essential to an America where every child will be educated and no child left behind.[20]

"There is no more powerful advocate for children than a parent armed with information and options."

—Rod Paige, U.S. Secretary of Education

Recommended publications for parents from the USDOE include:

Helping Your Child Succeed in School: Every child has the power to succeed in school and in life, and every parent, family member, and caregiver can help. This booklet provides parents with information, tools, and activities they can use in the home to help their child develop the skills critical to academic success.

[20]"Tools for Student Success." U.S. Department of Education. http://www.ed.gov/parents/academic/help/tools-for-success/index.html. 12/29/04.

Helping Your Child with Homework: Homework can help children develop positive study skills and habits, improve their thinking and memory abilities, and encourage them to use time well, learn independently, and take responsibility for their work. This booklet helps parents of elementary and junior high school students understand why homework is important and makes suggestions for helping children complete assignments successfully.

Helping Your Child Become a Reader: Other than helping your children to grow up healthy and happy, the most important thing that you can do for them is to help them develop their reading skills. This booklet offers pointers on how to build the language skills of young children and includes a list of typical language accomplishments for different age groups, suggestions for books, and resources for children with reading problems or learning disabilities.

Helping Your Child Become a Responsible Citizen: Just as children must be taught to read and write, solve math problems, and understand science concepts and events in history, so must they be guided in developing the qualities of character that are valued by their families and by the communities in which they live. This booklet provides information about the values and skills that make up character and good citizenship and what you can do to help your child develop strong character. It suggests activities that you and your school-aged children can do to put those values to work in your daily lives and tips for working with teachers and schools to ensure that you act together to promote the basic values that you want your child to learn and use.

Helping Your Child Learn Mathematics: Our increasingly technological world demands strong skills in mathematics not only in the workforce but also in everyday life, and these demands will only increase over the lifetimes of our children. The major portion of this booklet is made up of fun activities that parents can use with children from preschool age through grade 5 to strengthen their math skills and build strong positive attitudes toward math.

Helping Your Child Learn Science: Every day is filled with opportunities to learn science—without expensive chemistry sets or books. Parents don't need degrees in chemistry or physics to help their children learn science. All that is needed is a willingness to observe and learn with them and, above all, to make an effort and take the time to nurture their natural curiosity. This booklet provides parents of children ages 3 through 10 with information, tools, and activities they can use in the home and community to help their children develop an interest in the sciences and learn about the world around them.

Helping Your Child through Early Adolescence: Learning as much as you can about the world of early adolescents is an important step toward helping your child through the fascinating, confusing, and wonderful years from ages 10 through 14. Based on the latest research in adolescent development and learning, this booklet addresses questions, provides suggestions, and tackles issues that parents of young teens generally find most challenging.

Learn More Resource Center

http://www.learnmoreindiana.org
This is Indiana's pre-K to college connection. Information regarding how parents can help students in grades K-12, ways to support children's learning and academic development, college and career planning, and health is available.
Learn More Resource Center
2805 E. 10th Street
Bloomington, IN 47408
Toll-free helpline: (800) 992-2076

PRETEENS AND TEENS

What role do school and academics play in the life of your adolescents? Do they believe that education is important? How do they spend their time? Is most of their time spent participating in academic or school-related activities or in leisure activities? Are they involved in structured extracurricular activities? The answers to these questions contribute greatly to your adolescent's academic success.

The average American adolescents spend only 29 percent of their waking hours in school or school-related activities, compared with 40 percent in leisure activities, including socializing with friends, watching television, playing video games, etc. The remainder of adolescents' time (31 percent) is spent completing chores, working, and tending to maintenance activities such as personal hygiene.

In addition to adolescents spending less time in academic activities, the average adolescent also experiences a decrease in both academic achievement and motivation when he or she changes from elementary to middle school or junior high. Professionals believe this can be attributed to both the move to a new school and the secondary school environment itself. Adolescents need a supportive environment to develop their sense of independence, and the typical middle school and/or high school environment may not support this need. Instead, middle and high schools are often large and impersonal, lacking close relationships between students and teachers.

However, it is important for parents to know that the majority of adolescents do believe that education is important for success in life. This belief is usually stronger in adolescents whose parents emphasized the importance of education from an early age. Also, students who are involved in structured extracurricular activities *and* whose parents are involved in school and school-related activities are more likely to succeed academically and display fewer at-risk behaviors such as drug/alcohol abuse, truancy, sexual promiscuity, delinquent activity, etc.

Parents can help adolescents maintain their motivation to succeed in school during the transition to middle school and high school by:

- Continuing to emphasize the importance of education. Start in infancy and don't stop.
- Encouraging children to be involved in structured extracurricular activities. Adolescents who spend less unsupervised time perform better in school.
- Being involved with children's school and activities.

Several resources that are available to assist parents of adolescents include:

Learn More Resource Center
http://www.learnmoreindiana.org
This is Indiana's pre-K to college connection. Information regarding how parents can help students in grades 6-12, ways to support children's learning and academic development, college and career planning, and health is available. The Learn More Web site is underwritten by a grant from the Indiana Department of Workforce Development and is part of America's Career Resource Network (ACRN).
Learn More Resource Center
2805 E. 10th Street
Bloomington, IN 47408
Toll-free helpline: (800) 992-2076

The following article is reprinted from the Learn More Resource Center Web site.

10 Things Parents Can Do to Help Students Succeed[21]

1. **Promote college.** According to Indiana's new P-16 Plan for Improving Student Achievement, all students will need to keep learning after high school: at a two- or four-year college, at a trade school or apprenticeship program, or in the military. Otherwise, they will not have the knowledge and skills to get and keep a good job. Make sure that your middle school student knows that he or she will need to take Core 40 courses throughout high school, and explain why these higher expectations are so important for his or her future.
2. **Build relationships with your preteenager's teachers.** Find out what each teacher expects and how you can help your son or daughter prepare to meet those expectations. Make sure teachers and school counselors are promoting college, too.
3. **Read.** Reading is the foundation for all learning. Keep exposing your young person to a wide variety of reading materials (newspapers, magazines, books, Web), and be ready to discuss what he or she has learned. Helping him or her develop strong reading habits

[21]10 Things Parents Can Do to Help Students Succeed." Learn More Resource Center Web site. http://www.learnmoreindiana.org/@parents/parents_68/support_learning/quick_tips.xml. 12/29/04.

and skills is one of the most important contributions you can make to your child's education.

4. **Practice writing at home.** Letters, journal entries, e-mail messages, and grocery lists are all writing opportunities. Show that writing is an effective form of communication and that you write for a variety of purposes.
5. **Make math part of everyday life.** Cooking, gardening, paying bills, balancing a checkbook, and even shopping are all good ways to help your young person understand and use mathematics skills. Show that there may be many ways to get to the right answer, and encourage your son or daughter to explain his or her method.
6. **Expect that homework will be done.** Keep track of homework assignments, and regularly look at your student's completed work. Some teachers now give parents a number to call for a recorded message of that day's homework assignments; others put the information on the Internet. If your school doesn't offer these features, talk to the teacher about how you can get this important information. Even if there aren't specific assignments, find out how you can stay informed about what your young person is working on so that you can help at home.
7. **Use the community as a classroom.** Continue feeding your son's or daughter's curiosity about the world 365 days a year. Take him or her to museums, local government buildings, state parks, and workplaces. Encourage your student to volunteer in a field or area of interest in order to show how learning connects to the real world. These activities will reinforce what is learned in the classroom and may help your child decide what to do with his or her future.
8. **Encourage group study.** Open your home to your young person's friends for informal study sessions. Promote outside formal study groups through church or school organizations or other groups. Study groups will be especially important as your child becomes older and more independent. The study habits learned in middle school will carry over into college and work.
9. **Help other parents understand academic expectations.** Use your school and employee newsletters, athletic associations, booster clubs, a PTA or PTO meeting, or just a casual conversation to help other parents understand what academic standards mean for them, their children, and their school and how they can help their children learn at home. Also, make sure that other parents are promoting the college option, too. Remember, we want ALL children to have some college after high school. Now, of every 100 ninth graders, only 68 graduate from high school four years later, only 41 enter college,

and only 21 get a college degree within six years. That's not good enough if we want to keep our economy prosperous and our communities strong.

10. **Spend time at school.** The best way to know what goes on in your teenager's school is to spend time there. If you're a working parent, this isn't easy, and you may not be able to do it very often. But once in a while is better than never.

Extracurricular Activities for Teens

Most schools offer a wide variety of extracurricular programs. In addition, every community offers programs that emphasize the importance of both character and academic education. You might consider:

Youth as Resources of Central Indiana (YARCI)
United Way of Central Indiana
3901 N. Meridian Street
Indianapolis, IN 46208-0409
(317) 920-2562
Fax: (317) 921-1254
http://www.uwci.org/yar/
YAR is a community-based program providing small grants to young people (ages 5 to 21) to design and carry out service projects that address social problems and contribute to significant community change. Participants gain leadership, planning, teamwork, and other life skills; a sense of self-worth; accountability to the community; and pride in their accomplishments. There are 25 regional offices throughout Indiana. Call to find an office near you.

21st Century Scholars Statewide
815 W. Michigan Street, UC B-10
Indianapolis, IN
(317) 278-7589
http://www.scholars.indiana.edu
This program provides mentoring, support, and college tuition assistance (including academic workshops, college campus tours, parent support groups, tutoring, and in-school tracking as well as up to eight free semesters at a participating Indiana public college, university, or technical school). Participants must enroll in the seventh or eighth grade, meet income requirements, pledge to be crime, drug, and alcohol free, and maintain a 2.0 grade point average (GPA).

National Achievers Society
777 Indiana Avenue
Indianapolis, IN
(317) 693-7603
This educational program is for high school juniors and seniors with a GPA of 3.0 or above. NAS provides community service opportunities, college tours, competition for scholarships, and information regarding financial assistance. Urban League scholarships are also available to participants.

Indiana 4-H Extension Offices
http://www.four-h.purdue.edu
4-H provides fun, educational opportunities at the local, state, national, and international levels. 4-H programs are hands on, age appropriate, and university based. 4-H helps youth improve their self-confidence, learn subject matter, and develop important skills including leadership, citizenship, communication, and decision making that can be applied over a lifetime.

SPECIAL EDUCATION

The Americans with Disabilities Act of 1990 prohibits discrimination by state and federal government services solely on the basis of a disability. The Individuals with Disabilities Education Act of 1997 further expands the rights of students with disabilities. Indiana special education rules require that all students with disabilities who are enrolled in a public school be provided with a free, appropriate public education. As a result, special education services are provided at no extra cost and in ways that offer all students equal access to activities.

In most cases, students with special needs receive services within their regular general education classrooms at the school they attend. Special education and related services must be provided in the least restrictive environment (LRE). LRE means that a student with a disability participates in classes with students without disabilities as much as possible. Sometimes, students have needs that require services in specialized classrooms in another district school or other facility.

If your child is a preschooler and you suspect he or she may be developmentally delayed in one or more areas (such as speech, hearing, language, or motor skills), you should first talk with your pediatrician or family doctor. If special services are needed, you may want to contact the superintendent of your local school district or your district's director of special education.

For **older children already attending school**, you may discuss concerns about your child's achievement with the school counselor. The school counselor will work with you to determine whether additional testing is needed. There is no cost for testing to determine the need for special education services. A team of individuals, including parents, teachers, and others, will meet to review the test results. If necessary, a special education plan, called an individualized education plan (IEP), will be developed for your child. (See "Individualized Education Plan: Some Suggestions to Consider", **page 46.**)

If you are transferring your child with special needs from one school corporation to another, be sure to contact a guidance counselor in the new school to discuss your child's needs even before he or she is enrolled. This is helpful to the staff members who are working to make certain that everything is in place for your child to have a successful start in the new school. If your child already has an IEP, take a copy of the plan to the new school's counselor and request an IEP team meeting with the staff.

Many children diagnosed with a learning disability need extra help in special areas of learning. When you are looking for information, a good place to start is the **Yellow Pages for Kids with Disabilities** (http://www.yellowpagesforkids.com). This Web site lists many resources, including government programs, grassroots organizations, parent support groups, evaluators, educational consultants, academic tutors, advocates, and attorneys. The information is listed by state.

Exceptional Parent Magazine
http://www.eparent.com
"Information that matters from people who care" has been recognized as a leading resource for families with exceptional children. The magazine is available online and at newsstands.

Children with Disabilities under No Child Left Behind: Myths and Realities
http://www.wrightslaw.com/nclb/info/myths.ralities.napas.htm
This Web site includes an excellent paper by the National Association of Protection and Advocacy Systems (NAPAS) uncovering the myths that are being promoted by opponents of NCLB who suggest that students with disabilities are responsible for lowering school scores for AYP, causing schools to be "in need of improvement." The majority of special-needs students can succeed on standardized tests, and the new requirements of NCLB achieve the goal of drawing attention to students who were formerly "left behind."

Additional organizations that provide support for families:

Learning Disabilities Information and Referral
P.O. Box 20584
Indianapolis, IN 46220
Toll free: (800) 284-2519
This organization has information about local organizations that can provide help. It also makes referrals for testing, which is necessary to determine whether a child has a learning disability.

National Information Center for Children and Youth with Disabilities
P.O. Box 1492
Washington, D.C. 20013
Toll free: (800) 695-0285
http://www.nichcy.org
This organization provides information on disabilities and disability-related issues for families, educators, and other professionals. It offers personal responses to question through their free 800 number and has excellent publications.

Riley Hospital for Children: Camp Riley
Riley Memorial Association
50 S. Meridian Street, Suite 500
Indianapolis, IN 46202
(317) 634-4474
This organization offers a two-week summer camp for children and youth with physical disabilities. It offers boating, swimming, fishing, horseback riding, and a nature center; wooded trails are paved for wheelchairs. Financial assistance may be applied for.

ATTIC INC.
1721 Washington Avenue
Vincennes, IN 47591
(812) 886-0575
(800) 962-8842
http://www.theattic.org
ATTIC is a nonprofit, nonresidential, community-based, consumer-controlled, cross-disability organization that provides services and promotes activities to assist people with significant disabilities (and/or their families) in leading integrated, self-directed, and productive lives.

Programs for Infants and Toddlers with Disabilities: Ages Birth through 2
Assistant Deputy Director
Division of Family and Children/Bureau of Child Development
402 W. Washington Street, Room W-386
Indianapolis, IN 46204
(317) 232-2429
Fax: (317) 232-7948

Programs for Children with Disabilities: Ages 3 through 5
Project Coordinator
Division of Special Education
State Department of Education
State House, Room 229
Indianapolis, IN 46204-2798
(317) 232-057

Individualized Education Program (IEP): Some Suggestions to Consider[22]

Parents and professionals sometimes approach a child's individualized education program (IEP) meeting with mixed feelings. IEP team meetings, however, can be positive for both parties. The **Individuals with Disabilities Education Act (IDEA)** intended IEPs to be an opportunity for families and schools to work together to benefit each child with a disability.

A little background may put things into perspective:
Under IDEA, an evaluation determines whether a child is eligible for special education and related services. If the child is eligible, the law requires that a team of people (the IEP team) gathers to talk about what special instruction and services the child needs to succeed at school. This team must include the child's parent or legal guardian, as well as school staff and others as appropriate.

[22]"Individualized Education Program (IEP): Some Suggestions to Consider." *Exceptional Parent Magazine*. http://www.eparent.com/education/idea04_05.htm. 12/24/04.

The team members review information that tells them how the child is currently doing in school and his or her special needs. If the child has difficulty with reading, writing, paying attention, speaking, behaving appropriately, or other issues, the team decides what the child needs to work on during the year. Team decisions are written down, and the document is the individualized education program (IEP).

Preparing for an IEP meeting can equip a parent for discussion that will help keep the focus on his or her child. When a parent considers issues that may arise at the meeting and how he or she wishes to address them, it usually results in a more effective IEP.

Consider a variety of ways to involve your child in developing his or her IEP, starting at a young age if appropriate. Self-advocacy skills are important to develop.

Following are suggestions that may help parents prepare for the next IEP meeting.

Before the IEP team meeting:

- Consider the vision you have for your child for the future, as well as for the next school year.
- List your child's strengths, needs, and interests and your major concerns about his or her education.
- Consider how your child's disability affects his or her education.
- Think about your child's educational progress. What has worked and what has not?
- Request a written copy of your child's evaluation results or a meeting with school staff to discuss the evaluation before the IEP meeting. This gives you an opportunity to understand the evaluation before the IEP team meeting for your child.
- Consider the evaluation results. Do these results fit with what you know about your child? Is the evaluation complete and accurate? If you disagree with the school's evaluation, you may request, in writing, an independent educational evaluation (IEE), usually at no cost to you. The school must pay for the evaluation or show through a due process hearing that its evaluation is appropriate. The results of an IEP must be considered by the IEP team in planning your child's IEP.
- Consider a variety of ways to involve your child in developing his or her IEP, starting at a young age if appropriate. Self-advocacy skills are important to develop.
- If needed, plan to bring someone with you to the meeting with knowledge or special expertise regarding your child, such as a spouse, relative, friend, related service personnel, or representative from a local disability organization.

At the IEP team meeting:

The IEP meeting is very important. IEP team members attending the meeting will review and discuss information about the child at hand to develop the IEP. It provides an excellent opportunity to ask questions and share important insights about your child, whom you know better than anyone else does. The school needs to know what your child is like at home and in the community, as well as what your child's interests and activities are.

- Make sure others at the IEP meeting never forget that the meeting is about a real child—your child.
- Share your visions for your child, both short term and long term.
- Discuss your child's strengths and needs and any concerns about your child's education.
- Remember that diagnostic tests and assessments do not present the total picture.
- When you believe that the teacher and school personnel are doing a good job, tell them so. Praise, when deserved, is a great thing.
- Be a good listener. Ask questions.
- Make sure you understand. If you don't understand something, ask to have it explained in a way that you can understand.
- Expect that what you know about your child will be used in making decisions.
- Use school data, your child's progress reports, and other information you know about your child to make decisions.
- You may not want to agree to a proposed IEP at the end of the meeting. By law, you can review the proposed IEP document at home. If you disagree with what is being proposed in the IEP document, you must notify the school as soon as possible to resolve the disagreement.

After the IEP team meeting:

- Your child's IEP must be reviewed at least once a year to determine whether the annual goals have been achieved and to revise the IEP if necessary.
- Your child's school must inform you regularly about your child's progress, at least as often as parents who have children without disabilities are informed about the progress their children are making. Schools can do this by providing periodic report cards. You will be informed about whether your child is making progress toward meeting the annual IEP goals and whether the progress is enough to reach the goals. If your child is not making adequate progress, an IEP meeting should be called to review the IEP and make needed changes.
- You may request an IEP meeting at any time during the year if you believe it is important to consider changes in your child's IEP.

By law, you can review the proposed IEP document at home. If you disagree with what is being proposed in the IEP document, you must notify the school as soon as possible to resolve the disagreement.

PACER Center is a national training and information center for families of children and youth with all disabilities: physical, cognitive, learning, emotional, and others. ***PACER is located at 8161 Normandale Boulevard, Minneapolis, MN 55437-1044. Families can call (952) 838-9000, (952) 838-0190 (TTY), or (888) 248-0822 (toll free).*** *PACER's Web sites are http://www.pacer.org, http://www.taalliance.org, and http://www.fape.org, and its e-mail address is pacer@pacer.org.*

For a look at what the law says:
See the IDEA regulations Section 300.347 and Appendix A. The regulations are available online at http://www.access. gpo.gov/su_docs/fedreg/a990312c.html.

They are also available in hard copy at no charge from ED Pubs. Order online at http://www.edpubs.org or by phone at (877) 433-7827.

TUTORING PROGRAMS

In the past, private tutoring was reserved for kings and emperors who employed the best teachers and philosophers to privately educate their children. Private tutoring was available only to society's most privileged, ensuring that only the rich received the best education. However, today, many middle-class families are also enjoying the benefits of some form of private tutoring, and federal efforts are making tutoring available to the economically disadvantaged through a tutoring provision known as **supplemental educational services** (see **page 97**) established under President Bush's educational reform legislation, the No Child Left Behind Act of 2001.

Tutoring can be used to help students who have performed poorly on yearly standardized tests; to help ensure that elementary school students master basic skills before more complex ideas are introduced or to help them prepare for mandatory end-of-year standardized testing; to help students who are having difficulty with a particular subject; and to help students with learning disabilities master subjects and study skills.

The **goal of tutoring** for remedial purposes is to teach the student *how to learn* the subject for which he or she is being tutored so that the student ultimately no longer needs the assistance of the tutor. For tutoring to be successful, two things must take place. First, students must attend school and their tutoring sessions. Second, tutors should be educated and trained in both the subject matter for which they are tutoring and strategic tutoring methods. Although the time required for each student to master skills varies, results from tutoring can be expected within eight to 10 weeks of individualized one-on-one tutoring sessions occurring at least one hour per week.

FREE Tutoring

Many community centers, faith-based organizations, Boys and Girls Clubs, and other service organizations offer free tutoring. In the Indianapolis area, more than 30 organizations offer free or low-cost tutoring.

Students may be eligible for free tutoring through their public school if they currently attend a school designated by the state for two years in a row as "in need of improvement." These schools are required to spend some of the Title I funds they received from the federal government to provide disadvantaged students with free tutoring or supplemental educational services. To see whether your school is required to provide free tutoring, see the GEO foundation Web site, http://www.geofoundation.org. If your student is eligible for tutoring, the list of approved tutors can be found on the Web site of the Indiana Department of Education at http://www.doe.state.in.us/esea/pdf/SESApprList-2004-06.pdf.

Tutoring Programs

Indiana Reading Corps
The Indiana Reading Corps program tutors K-6 children in 92 Indiana schools. Using planned one-on-one tutoring sessions up to three times a week, focused around quality children's literature, activities following the session are designed to improve comprehension, communication, and writing skills. Volunteer tutors include college students and community members. Utilizing this one-on-one model, results have shown an increase in children's literacy rates statewide, overall classroom confidence, self-esteem levels, and community engagement.

Call the state office for information at (317) 274-6500, or visit http://www.indianacampuscompact.org/.

There are also a wealth of new tutoring resources available online. Many of these services are not free, but they may be cost effective when you consider that they are accessible from your own home. For a start, you might consider:

Homework Hotline
http://www.askrose.org
(877) ASK-ROSE
Rose-Hulman Institute of Technology's Homework Hotline is a **free math and science tutoring** service for Indiana middle and high school students, funded by Lilly Endowment, 3M Corporation, and Rose Hulman. A free community service since 1991, **the program provides tutoring via a toll-free phone call.** The Homework Hotline reinforces math and science concepts and helps students develop better problem-solving skills. Tutors answer calls between 7 p.m. and 10 p.m. (EST), Sunday through Thursday, from September through May. Homework Hotline tutors guide students in learning more about a subject but do not do the work for them. Tutors are trained to ask the right questions to help students analyze the problems and find their own solutions.

Online Tutoring in Indiana
http://www.anysubject.com/us/Indiana.htm
This online tutoring program offers classes at every level from elementary through college and employs a variety of educators to provide tutoring. The fee for this online tutoring program is $30 per hour.

Tutor.com
http://www.tutor.com
Founded in partnership with the *Princeton Review*, Tutor.com is the leading provider of online tutoring services for education institutions and individual students. Tutor.com provides a 24-hour, one-to-one online tutoring service

delivered via its proprietary Online Classroom, utilizing the Web's largest network of tutors, and supported by powerful administrative and reporting tools. The Tutor.com Online Classroom enables learners and tutors to interact in a variety of ways, including speaking to each other live, using whiteboard technology, sharing documents, and chatting and browsing the Web together. There is a fee for this service, starting at $20 per hour.

Young Child Education: Games and Online Tutoring
http://www.young-child-education.org/
One of the best ways for your children to learn is from the comfort of their own home with fun yet educational games and online tutoring. With interactive math and reading games, your children will actually look forward to learning and will gain the confidence and skills to get ahead in school. Online tutoring allows your children to become efficient with a computer at an early age at the same time they receive their interactive expert help with lessons.

PLANNING FOR HIGH SCHOOL

For parents, a child's education is a major investment of time and energy. Parents spend years making sure that their child attends school regularly and helping with homework, meeting with teachers, and providing extracurricular opportunities. The elementary and preteen years go by quickly, and before you know it, your teen is ready for high school.

High school is an exciting, stressful, and important time for both teenagers and parents. In addition to all the social stress of the teenage years, high school students must start preparing for their future and making plans for life after graduation. The following information will help parents and students make the most out of the high school years and prepare effectively for college.

As a parent, you can help your student prepare for high school by doing your research and learning all you can about the high school your child will be attending. Courses and requirements may have changed since you last attended high school. Do you know what tests must be passed in order to graduate? What high school courses best prepare your teen for college? What your teen's interests are? What his or her plans are beyond high school? Do not wait until your student is in the eleventh or twelfth grade to begin thinking about the future; *the journey to adulthood officially begins on the first day of high school*!

Graduation Qualifying Exam (GQE)

All students are required to demonstrate that they have met the achievement standards measured by the ISTEP+ Graduation Qualifying Exam (GQE) in order to graduate. Tenth-grade students in Indiana's public and accredited nonpublic high schools take the ISTEP+ GQE. Beginning in fall 2004, incoming Indiana sophomores will take a new version of the GQE. The GQE is a continuation of the ISTEP+ program, and students must pass to graduate.[23] The test is made up of two sections and tests grade 9 English/language arts, K-8 mathematics, and Algebra I standards. Students are tested to guarantee that they have mastered the skills they need to compete successfully in an increasingly demanding world before they graduate from high school. The test also helps schools identify students who need additional help in reading, writing, and mathematics.

The Indiana Department of Education recommends that students prepare to reach higher standards, especially in math, so all students are encouraged to take Algebra I no later than their freshman year. Algebra is sometimes called a "gateway" course because students need algebra for admission to college and trade schools.

[23]Students with special needs may qualify for a waiver. Contact your school for more information.

What if the student doesn't pass the GQE?

Sophomore students who do not pass the GQE in the fall will be given four other opportunities to take the exam, twice a year in their junior and senior years. If your student does not pass the GQE, your school has resources to provide remedial help. Schools receive money to provide remediation services to all students who do not score at or above the passing score. It is primarily the school's responsibility to provide remedial assistance to students. But it is up to the students and parents to take advantage of the assistance available.

Special Education

If your son or daughter receives instructional or testing accommodations, these should be specified in the individualized education program (IEP) or Section 504 Plan. (See **page 46**) Many of these accommodations are allowed during ISTEP+ testing. If a student's case conference committee determines that the GQE is not an appropriate test for a student, then the student should participate in an alternate assessment. Participating in an alternate assessment does not qualify a student for meeting the GQE requirement necessary for a diploma. The **Indiana Standards Tool for Alternate Reporting** (ISTAR) is the alternate assessment component in Indiana's statewide system of accountability. It is available free of charge to all educators in accredited schools throughout Indiana. Contact your son's or daughter's school for more information or go to http://doe.state.in.us/exceptional/speced/whatsnew.html.

For more information about the GQE, see **page 53**, or go to sites:

ISTEP+ Info Center:
http://www.doe.state.in.us/istep

Indiana Academic Standards:
http://www.doe.state.in.us/standards

Core 40/Graduation Requirements

Core 40 is a single, flexible high school curriculum that, except for electives, has been determined to best prepare a student for the workforce or postsecondary education. This curriculum is the standard for college admission at Indiana colleges and universities.

Core 40 requirements include:

- 4 years of language arts
- 3 years of science

- 3 years of social studies
- 3 years of mathematics
- 1 semester of physical education
- 1 semester of health
- Additional electives in the areas of computer technology, foreign language, arts, and career-area subjects

This should total 40 semester credits.

Although this is the standard for Indiana, some colleges require more in certain subject areas (example: two years in a foreign language or two years in a specific laboratory science). *Plan ahead and research the colleges your student may want to attend to determine their specific requirements.*

The following is a more specific breakdown of a typical program that meets Core 40 requirements[24]:

Language arts:	8 credits in literature, composition, and speech
Math:	6 to 8 credits in Algebra I, geometry, Algebra II, trigonometry, and calculus
Science:	6 credits in laboratory science from the following: 2 credits biology and 2 credits in chemistry or physics and 2 additional credits from chemistry, physics, earth/space science, advanced biology, advanced chemistry, advanced physics, or advanced environmental science
Social studies:	6 credits distributed as follows: 2 credits in U.S. history 1 credit in U.S. government 1 credit in economics 1 credit in world history and civilization or world geography 1 additional course from above or other social studies area
Physical education:	1 credit
Health/safety:	1 credit
	8 additional credits from the list above or foreign language, arts, computers, or a career area 2 to 4 credits from any course

[24]1 credit = 1 semester

Career and Technical Education

Students who do not plan to attend college may be interested in career and technical education. Career and technical education courses help students explore their interests and career possibilities and prepare for a career of interest. The content of career and technical education courses includes academic subject matter taught with relevance to the real world, job-related activities, and workplace ethics. In some areas of the state, school districts provide career and technical education through regional-area career centers.

In Indiana, career and technical education courses fall within six different program areas:

- **Administration and finance education**
  http://www.doe.state.in.us/octe/admin_finance/welcome.html
- **Agriculture education**
  http://www.doe.state.in.us/octe/ag_ed/welcome.html
- **Business and marketing education**
  http://www.doe.state.in.us/octe/bme/welcome.html
- **Family and consumer science**
  http://www.doe.state.in.us/octe/facs/welcome.html
- **Health occupations**
  http://www.doe.state.in.us/octe/health/welcome.html
- **Technology education**
  http://www.doe.state.in.us/octe/technologyed/welcome.html

Working and High School

Working after school or on weekends helps a teen develop maturity and independence. Working can provide extra money for clothing or college and can offer some real-world experience. Unfortunately, a job can also distract a teen from his or her primary responsibility—graduating from high school and preparing for the future.

Before a teen starts a new job, there are several things to consider:

- **Work permit:** In Indiana, all teens 14, 15, 16, and 17 years of age who do not have a high school or GED diploma must have a work permit before starting work. Work permits can be obtained from your local high school.
- **Work schedule:** Talk with your student and agree upon the time the job will require and how it will affect the amount of time needed for schoolwork.
- **Monitor your student's grades.** Make sure the student understands that school comes first, and evaluate his or her ability to manage a job and schoolwork.

For more information:
The Teen Worker Web site at http://www.in.gov/labor/childlabor/, developed by the Indiana Bureau of Child Labor, is a one-stop guide to Indiana's teen work (child labor) laws. This easy-to-use Web site contains all the information you need to know about Indiana's teen work laws and contains up-to-date publications, forms, news, and statistics about Indiana's teen workforce. This site is designed to help guide teens, parents, employers, and educators in their understanding of Indiana's teen work laws. Teens are encouraged to use this site to learn their rights and obligations under Indiana's teen work laws.

Bureau of Child Labor
Indiana Department of Labor
402 W. Washington Street, Room W195
Indianapolis, IN 46204
Phone Numbers:
Local: (317) 232-2675
Toll free: (888) TEEN-WORK
Fax: (317) 233-3790

Preparing for Life after High School

General Educational Diploma

A **General Educational Diploma**, known as the **GED**, offers adults a "second chance" to earn high school credentials. More than 14 million adults have received GED diplomas since 1949.

A person who is at least 17 years of age may be eligible to take the GED. However, the average age of participants taking the test continues to be between 24 and 25 years of age. Indiana's oldest graduate last year, and possibly the oldest in the history of our state's GED testing, was a 91-year-old woman who enrolled in college after receiving her GED.

The exam is comprised of five subjects: writing skills, social studies, science, interpreting literature and the arts, and mathematics. Each person who takes and passes the GED exceeds the performance of at least one-third of the nation's high school seniors. The test itself is based on twelfth-grade standards while the Graduation Qualification Exam (GQE) is based only on standards for the ninth grade.

More than 70 percent of people who took the exam said they were taking the GED to qualify for further education. Another 42 percent indicated they wanted *better* jobs, and several wanted to qualify for the military. The majority of all adults who applied for the GED reported they had completed tenth grade or higher before leaving the traditional high school.[25]

[25]"GED Opens Doors for Hoosiers." Indiana Department of Education.

Interesting facts from the Possibility Network (http://www.Indianalearn.com):

- GED recipients outperform traditional high school graduating seniors by 40 percent.
- 97 percent of colleges and universities accept GED diplomas.
- More than 90 percent of U.S. employers consider GED recipients the same as traditional high school graduates with regards to hiring, salary, and opportunity for advancement.
- In regards to high school level education in Indiana, 10.6 percent of people in the overall population are GED recipients while the rest are high school graduates.

To obtain more information about the GED, call the **Indiana Department of Education Division of Adult Education,** (317) 232-0522, or visit the **American Council on Education** Web site, http://www.acenet.edu.

Additional sources of GED information are listed below:

GED on TV (Indiana Learn at Home)
(877) GED-ONTV or (877) 433-6688
GED preparation classes are available through Indiana Public Broadcasting Stations.

Hispanic Education Center: GED
580 E. Stevens Street
Indianapolis, IN 46203
(317) 634-5022
This organization offers GED preparation in a class setting.

There are more than 70 testing centers in Indiana. They can be found in high schools, vocational school facilities, or career centers. Be sure to call for the testing site schedule. Each testing center sets its own schedule. It is best to register and pay ahead of the test. For a listing of sites, call (317) 232-0522 or visit the Web site http://ideanet.doe.state.in.us/adulted/ged.htm.

Vocational Schools

Career and Technical Education

Career and technical education courses help students explore their interests and career possibilities and prepare for a career of interest. The content of career and technical education courses includes academic subject matter taught with relevance to the real world, job-related activities, and workplace ethics. In some areas of the state, school districts provide career and technical education through regional-area career centers.

In Indiana, career and technical education courses fall within six different program areas:

- **Administration and finance education**
  http://www.doe.state.in.us/octe/admin_finance/welcome.html
- **Agriculture education**
  http://www.doe.state.in.us/octe/ag_ed/welcome.html
- **Business and marketing education**
  http://www.doe.state.in.us/octe/bme/welcome.html
- **Family and consumer science**
  http://www.doe.state.in.us/octe/facs/welcome.html
- **Health occupations**
  http://www.doe.state.in.us/octe/health/welcome.html
- **Technology education**
  http://www.doe.state.in.us/octe/technologyed/welcome.html

Job Corps

Job Corps is a no-cost education and vocational training program administered by the U.S. Department of Labor that helps young people ages 16 through 24 get a better job, make more money, and take control of their lives.

At Job Corps, students enroll to learn a trade, earn a high school diploma or GED, and get help finding a good job. When students join the program, they will be paid a monthly allowance; the longer they stay with the program, the more their allowance will be. Job Corps supports its students for up to 12 months after they graduate from the program.

To enroll in Job Corps, students must meet the following requirements:

- Be 16 through 24.
- Be a U.S. citizen or legal resident.
- Meet income requirements.
- Be ready, willing, and able to participate fully in an educational environment.

Funded by the U.S. Congress, Job Corps has been training young adults for meaningful careers since 1964. Job Corps is committed to offering all students a safe, drug-free environment where they can take advantage of the resources provided.

If you're interested in joining the Job Corps program or finding out more about it, call (800) 733-JOBS (800-733-5627). An operator will provide you with general information about the program, refer you to the admissions counselor closest to where you live, and mail you an information packet. Additional information regarding the Indiana Job Corps sites is available at http://www.jobcorps.doleta.gov/centers/in.cfm.

Vocational School Education

Vocational schools provide specialized education for students interested in pursuing a vocation immediately upon graduation from high school. Apprenticeship or intern experiences are commonly part of the education. Vocational choices often include health or technology options.

For information on Indiana vocational schools, log onto http://www.vocational-schools.info/Vocational-Schools-in-Indiana.htm or My Career Education, http://www.my-career-education.com/indiana.htm.

Military Training

Joining the military offers students an opportunity to gain specific job skills and experience, great work habits, job-related higher education, and savings for college. The U.S. military has five separate services: the Army, Navy, Marine Corps, Air Force, and Coast Guard. The Army, Navy, and Air Force are among the largest employers in the country.

You can find out what it's like to be a soldier, what military jobs are available, and the benefits of joining the military through the following contacts.

U.S. Army: http://www.goarmy.com, (800) USA-ARMY, ext. 181
U.S. Coast Guard: http://www.gocoastguard.com, (877) NOW-USCG (877-669-8724)
U.S. Marines: http://www.marines.com, (800) MARINES
U.S. National Guard: http://www.1800goguard.com, (800) GO GUARD
U.S. Navy: http://www.navy.com, (800) USA-NAVY

Preparing for College

According to the Indiana Association of College Admission Counselors, a high school program that meets requirements for college admission includes:

College-prep English:	4 years including grammar, literature, and composition
College-prep math:	3 to 4 years including algebra, geometry, and advanced algebra
Laboratory science:	2 to 3 years of biology, chemistry, and/or physics
Social sciences:	2 years of U.S. history, world history, government, sociology, psychology, economics
Introductory courses:	Experience with music and/or art
Skills courses:	Experience with typing and basic computer skills

College Admissions Tests

Most colleges and universities require standardized admissions tests as part of the application process. Students who think they may want to go to college should keep this door open by taking advantage of practice standardized college admissions tests early in their high school years. They also need to be aware of test application deadlines for the actual admissions tests. Students should find out which test is required by the colleges to which they plan to apply.

PLAN

PLAN is a pre-ACT test typically administered in the sophomore year of high school. It helps students measure their current academic development so they can plan for the remaining years of high school. For more information, log onto http://www.act.org/plan/index.html.

ACT

The ACT test is often required by Southern and Midwestern colleges and universities. The test is 3 hours and 30 minutes long and measures English, math, science, reading, and writing skills. Many free resources are available to help students prepare for the test.

To apply, call ACT Inc. at (319) 337-1270.

Register online at http://www.act.org or ask about the test at an area high school.

Prescholastic Aptitude Test (PSAT)

A shorter practice version of the Scholastic Aptitude Test (SAT), the PSAT can be help students to become more comfortable with the testing process. PSAT scores will inform the students of areas for improvement prior to taking the SAT, the test that becomes part of students' college application. Preparation resources include free services such as the "Word du Jour" daily vocabulary service and strategy seminars and fee-based tutoring and online courses.

Scholastic Aptitude Test (SAT)

The SAT is the oldest and best-known standardized college admission test. It is commonly required of East and West Coast schools. The current test is 3 hours long and tests verbal and math skills. The new version available in 2005 will be 3 hours and 45 minutes long and will include critical reading, math, and writing sections. Students achieving high scores on the test may qualify for National Merit Scholarships and Letters of Commendation. Many free resources are available to help students prepare for the test. To apply for the test, log onto http://www.collegeboard.com or ask about the test at an area high school.

SAT II

The SAT II is the new name for what were formerly Achievement Tests. These tests are subject specific for math, chemistry, Spanish, history, and more. Many competitive schools require students to submit up to three subject-specific scores along with the overall SAT score. Check with the colleges to which you are applying and ask which if any SAT II scores they require.

For more information about any of these tests, visit http://www.princetonreview.com/college/testprep/.

Effective preparation for college begins in the ninth grade.

Ninth grade is the official beginning of "high school," and colleges consider grades and extracurricular activities from the ninth through twelfth grades when reviewing applications for admission. Below is a timeline for effective college planning:

Ninth grade

Fall:

- Take the most challenging courses available
- Join clubs/activities in areas of interest
- Build relationships with peers, teachers, counselors, activity coordinators, and employers (these individuals will be writing recommendations for you in a few years)
- Select and participate in a service area
- Develop good study habits

Spring:

- Job shadow or participate in a career day in areas of interest
- Begin constructing a résumé
- Discuss post-high school plans with school counselor and parent/guardian
- Begin to discuss college costs with parent/guardian

Tenth grade

Fall:

- Take the most challenging courses of study available
- Look for leadership roles in clubs/activities
- Continue development of service activity
- Strengthen relationship with peers, teachers, counselors, activity moderators, and employers
- Test preparation: Take the pre-SAT (PSAT) or the ACT preparation called PLAN
- Attend college fairs (see section on college fairs for some tips)
- Continue working on study habits and note-taking skills

Spring:
- Job shadow or participate in a career day
- Review and update résumé
- Continue discussing post–high school plans with school counselor and parent/guardian
- Review college costs and explore options

Eleventh grade
Fall:
- Take the most challenging courses of study available
- Demonstrate leadership and responsibility in community and school
- Begin a list of colleges of interest
- Gather information about careers of interest (i.e., educational requirements, demand, etc.)
- Make the most out of a part-time job (i.e., try to select a part-time job related to career interests)
- Talk with college representatives and ask questions
- Attend local information sessions about college
- Attend college fairs
- Discuss testing plans with school counselor and allow time to retake tests if needed
- Register, prepare for, and take the PSAT
- Begin free scholarship searches
- Visit colleges (see section for tips on making the most out of college visits)
- Begin considering who will write college recommendations
- Continue talking about your plans with parents and school counselor

March:
- Request information from colleges (i.e., admission packet)
- Take SAT; information about the SAT can be found at http://www.makingcollegecount.com
- Visit colleges during spring break
- Research scholarship opportunities
- Discuss college financial costs with parents/guardians
- Meet with college financial aid representative

April:
- Take ACT; information about the ACT can be found at http://www.makingcollegecount.com
- Attend college fairs
- Look for summer job (preferably related to career interest)

May:
- Take the SAT
- Finalize summer plans

June-August:
- Retake SAT/ACT if needed
- Update résumé
- Save money for college costs
- Request scholarship applications

Twelfth grade

September:
- Talk with counselors and parents/guardians about plans
- Visit college representatives
- Request college information, including financial aid and housing
- Begin processing applications and keep copies for your records
- Write essays needed for applications and request recommendations
- Send test scores/transcripts to colleges you are interested in
- Request financial aid applications
- Meet all deadlines

October:
- Take ACT if needed

November:
- Obtain FAFSA form for financial aid
  More information and the **FREE** Application for Federal Student Aid are available from the U.S. Department of Education online at http://www.fafsa.ed.gov.

December:
- Finish applications

January:
- Rank schools in order of preference (based on information obtained from information sessions, campus visits, etc.)
  Get financial information in order and complete the FAFSA before February 1. A checklist is available from **Indiana College Answer**, http://www.indiana.collegeanswer.com.

February-March:
- Keep your grades up; colleges/universities consider all grades from ninth through twelfth grades but place greater importance on later grades
- Review financial aid information

April:
- Visit colleges
- Make final decision about which college to attend
- Contact financial aid office

May-June:
- Follow procedure for orientation
- Plan and budget college expenses

College Fairs

Each school year, a number of college fairs are held in Indiana. College fairs are an excellent opportunity for colleges and universities to recruit prospective new students and, more important, for students to learn about colleges/universities by asking questions and interacting with representatives. Below are some suggestions on how to get the most out of college fairs.

Before the college fair:

- Review information about the colleges/universities that are participating in the college fair. Information about colleges/universities can be found in books such as *Peterson's Four-Year Colleges* and similar books published by Kaplan and the Princeton Review. Most schools also have Web sites.
- Locate the schools you are interested in.
- Check out the schedule of information sessions.

Admissions Questions

- What are the admission requirements?
- What are the required standardized test scores (i.e., SAT and ACT scores)?
- What majors does the school offer? What are the most popular majors?
- When is the application deadline?
- Are interviews required for admission? Are the interviews group or individual interviews?
- How can I arrange a campus visit?
- After an application is submitted, how long will it be before a decision is made?

Financial Aid Questions

- What is the cost of the college/university?
- What are the financial aid options?
- When is the deadline for applying for financial aid?
- What percentage of work study, loans, grants, and scholarships is awarded in the college/university's financial aid packets?

For financial aid deadlines, log onto the Federal Student Aid Web site at http://www.fafsa.ed.gov/index.htm.

Classroom/Academic Questions

- What is the average class size?
- Are professors easily accessible?
- Do professors or graduate students teach courses?
- When must a major be declared?
- Is a personal computer needed?
- What student services are available? (tutoring, career counseling, etc.)
- What facilities are available, such as libraries, computer labs, etc.?

Housing Questions

- What types of housing are available?
- Are roommates required?
- If so, how are roommates selected?

Student Life Questions

- What groups exist on campus? Fraternities and sororities?
- What weekend activities are available?
- Are intramural sports available?
- What are the meal plan options?

Miscellaneous Questions

- How many freshmen return as sophomores?
- What is done to insure students' safety on campus?

College Visits

Most colleges and universities offer prospective new students special days when they visit the campus in a large group and take tours and attend information sessions. These visits are helpful in the beginning of the decision-making process. However, after the choices have been narrowed down, it is important to schedule an individual campus visit if possible. This provides the opportunity to meet one on one with admissions staff, academic advisors, financial aid advisors, professors, and students. Most schools are usually willing to allow prospective students to attend classes related to their area of interest. High school juniors and seniors are typically encouraged to visit colleges, and most high schools acknowledge college visitation days as excused absences. You'll want to check with your school to see how many days are available. Spring break is a great time to visit colleges, too!

Important questions to ask when visiting colleges and universities:

- Is it easy to get around campus? Can I walk to and from classes?
- Where is the central gathering place for students?
- Is the campus self-contained or fairly spread out?
- How are the dormitories segregated? By class? Gender? Major?
- What means of transportation are available to go off campus?
- Are the facilities relatively new?
- What do students do on the weekends? Are there on-/off-campus activities?
- What safety measures are utilized? Are there campus police? Is the blue light system used? Does the school offer walking escorts? Are IDs checked to enter residential buildings?

More questions and answers can be found at http://www.makingcollegecount.com.

College Preparation Programs

Many students find it helpful to prepare for college in a more hands-on manner. In Indiana, many colleges and universities allow high school students to take college courses that count for both high school and college credits. Some of the participating schools are:

- Indiana University
- Purdue University
- Indiana University Purdue University at Indianapolis (IUPUI)
- Taylor University
- Ivy Tech
- Others—contact the individual school for more information

21st Century Scholars
This statewide program provides mentoring, support, and college tuition assistance for seventh and eighth graders who meet certain requirements, such as income requirements, pledging to be crime, drug, and alcohol free, and maintaining a 2.0 GPA throughout high school. Representatives from 21st Century Scholars follow the youth through high school and offer academic workshops, college campus tours, parent support groups, and tutoring. Information can be obtained from school guidance counselor or directly from the organization.

21st Century Scholars
815 W. Michigan Street
UC B-10
Indianapolis, IN 46202
(317) 278-7589
http://www.scholars.indiana.edu

Scholarships

Here are some helpful Web sites to assist in a scholarship search.

Black Excel
http://www.blackexcel.org/100minority.htm
This site provides information about more than 1,000 scholarships for minorities.

Central Indiana Community Foundation (CICF)
http://www.cifc.org/Scholarships/
This site sponsors scholarship endowments for students in central Indiana. This Web site also provides valuable information about college, financial aid, and scholarship searches beyond this program. The link for scholarships sponsored by CICF is http://www.cicf.org/Scholarships/PDF/Scholarship_Booklet.pdf.

Kohl's Kids Who Care Program
http://www.kohlscorporation.com/CommunityRelations/Community02.htm
This program rewards youth who volunteer in their community.

Simon Youth Foundation
http://syf.simon.com/syf.aspx?pgID=438
This foundation awards community scholarships for high school seniors planning to attend a two- or four-year accredited institution. Applications may be picked up at area Simon malls in the fall. The deadline for application is in February.

State Student Assistance Commission of Indiana (SSACI)
http://www.ai.org/ssaci/programs/index.html
This program offers scholarship/grant programs for Indiana students and links to other sites offering scholarships and grants.

USA Funds Access to Education Scholarships
This program offers scholarships for high school seniors and current college students who have a family income of $35,000 or less. Fifty percent of awards are given to minority and disabled students.

The following is a list of other helpful Web sites to get you started in your search for scholarship and financial aid:

FastWeb: http://www.fastweb.monster.com
College Board Scholarship Search: http://www.collegeboard.com
GoCollege: http://www.gocollege.com
Indiana Wired Scholar: http://www.indiana.wiredscholar.com
Free Scholarships: http://www.freescholarshipguide.com. This site publishes a directory of 4,000 Web sites where you can search for scholarships.
Get College Funds: http://www.getcollegefunds.org

ADULT EDUCATION

A quality education is just as important for adults as it is for children, and it is never too late to learn. Below is information for statewide programs that offer adult education according to your individual learning needs, from literacy education to college courses.

Indiana Literacy Foundation
1920 W. Morris Street
Indianapolis, IN 46221
(317) 639-6106 ext. 211
http://www.indianaliteracy.org
This foundation operates the Literacy Help Line at (317) 636-6106 ext. 211, a central referral network that refers to local literacy programs throughout Indiana.

Even Start Family Literacy
3650 Cold Springs Road
Indianapolis, IN 46222
(317) 226-3275
This is a family-focused program that allows parents and children to attend school together. Key components include adult literacy, preschool education, and parenting education. Participants must live in the Indianapolis Public School district and have children ages 0 to 8. It is free. Transportation is provided.

Goodwill Industries of Central Indiana
1635 W. Michigan Street
Indianapolis, IN
(317) 264-1315
http://www.goodwill-indy.org/education.htm
This program provides adult basic education, GED preparation, and English as a Second Language education. It also offers employment assistance and job opportunities and serves individuals 16 and older. To find a Goodwill Industries near you, log onto http://www.locator.goodwill.org.

Indiana Learn at Home
2500 N. Elgin Street
Muncie, IN
(765) 747-5353
(877) 433-6688

GED on TV
http://www.gedontv.org
To enroll, call (877) 433-6688 weekdays. This program provides GED preparation classes via the Indiana Public Broadcasting Stations. It provides workbooks, a toll-free help line, an official GED calculator, and a practice test. Participants earn a $45 voucher to pay for the GED test at any Indiana test site. The multimedia series includes 39 half-hour TV programs that cover the reading, writing, social studies, science, and math skills adults need to brush up on to pass the GED high school equivalency tests. Two five-month "semesters" of two lessons per week are shown each year.

Hoosier adults 17 years and older may enroll by toll-free telephone and receive books by UPS. The cost to the student is $45, which covers pre- and post-testing, three workbooks, the official GED calculator, and a voucher to pay for the GED test at any Indiana GED testing site. In Indiana, GED testing costs up to $60. Each adult who enrolls takes a pretest at home to determine what he or she needs to study. Students with low reading levels or math levels will be referred to an adult learning center in their home community. Most successful students read at the tenth grade level before they begin to study from home. Some adults pretest with very high scores, and they are encouraged to take the GED practice test and the GED right away.

Since the GED on TV program expanded statewide in 1990–1991, nearly 7,000 adults have earned a GED diploma after watching the program from home. Students have ranged in age from 17 to 92 and are 74 percent women. The average last grade completed was tenth grade.

Indiana Department of Education: Division of Adult Education
(317) 232-0522
http://doe.state.in.us/adulted/welcome.html
The IDOE produces a comprehensive directory of adult education programs organized by counties and regions throughout the state.

Office of Vocational and Adult Education
http://www.ed.gov
The federal Office of Vocational and Adult Education (OVAE) in the U.S. Department of Education works to ensure that all Americans have the knowledge and technical skills necessary to succeed in postsecondary education, the workforce, and life. Through the Preparing America's Future initiative's comprehensive policies, programs, and activities, OVAE is helping reform America's high schools, supporting America's community colleges, and expanding America's adult education programs. The federal government provides funds for many local adult education programs.

The Possibility Network
http://www.indianalearn.com
This site lists career, learning, finance, and community information for Indiana, which includes a listing of higher education degree programs and financial assistance information.

Colleges and Universities
Colleges and universities throughout Indiana offer evening, and sometimes weekend, courses to accommodate working adults' schedules. Check with your local college, university, or technical school for more information.

Learn More Resource Center

The **Learn More Resource Center** is Indiana's new, expanded pre-K to college connection. The successor to the Indiana Career and Postsecondary Advancement Center (ICPAC), Learn More was created to support the Indiana Education Roundtable's P-16 Plan for Improving Student Achievement. The plan's key principle is that in today's world, Indiana students need successfully to COMPLETE postsecondary education.

With Indiana's P-16 plan as its foundation, the Learn More Resource Center strives to be the most valuable and reliable source of information for Indiana's parents, students, and school counselors. Learn More also serves adults who want to change careers or seek additional training.

Since its inception in 1986, ICPAC provided unrivaled support and guidance to Indiana's high school students. In just over a decade, Indiana improved its participation in postsecondary education from less than 37 percent in 1986 to more than 61 percent today and improved its ranking from fortieth to seventeenth in the nation.

ICPAC's success was based on the premise that students and their families need to receive key guidance messages at appropriate times. The same principle remains as a solid nucleus of Learn More.

Contact Information
Learn More Resource Center (Learn More)
2805 E. 10th Street
Bloomington, IN 47408
Toll-free helpline: (800) 992-2076, Monday-Friday, 8 a.m.–7 p.m.
Fax: (812) 855-4220

"EDUCATIONAL AND FUN" FIELD TRIPS

Of all the teachers your child will ever have, the most influential—and probably their favorite—will be you! You are teaching your children at all times, and they are learning all the time, whether in a formal classroom, in your home, or at the zoo! In Indiana, there are many opportunities to combine family fun and learning experiences. Taking your children on family field trips enables them to have hands-on experiences that enhance the things they learn from books or in the classroom. Many of these outings are free or very low cost. It's always a good idea to call first and find out pertinent information such as hours of operation and when tours are available. Some suggestions to get you started:

Arts

Asante Children's Theatre
502 N. Tremont
Indianapolis, IN
(317) 635-7211 ext. 228

Buck Creek Players Theater
7820 Acton Road
Indianapolis, IN
(317) 862-2270

Dance Kaleidoscope
429 E. Vermont
Indianapolis, IN
(317) 634-8484

Eiteljorg Museum of the American Indian and Western Art
500 W. Washington Street
Indianapolis, IN
(317) 636-9378

Indianapolis Children's Theatre
1005 Woodmere Drive
Indianapolis, IN
(317) 253-8380

Madame Walker Theatre
617 Indiana Avenue
Indianapolis, IN
(317) 236-2099

National Art Museum of Sport
111 Monument Circle
Indianapolis, IN
(317) 687-1715

Philharmonic Orchestra of Indpls
17 W. Market Street
Indianapolis, IN
(317) 283-5242

T.C. Steele State Historic Site
(812) 988-2785

Museums and History

Indianapolis Museum of Art
1200 W. 38th Street
Indianapolis, IN
(317) 923-1331

Indiana Repertory Theatre
140 W. Washington Street
Indianapolis, IN
(317) 253-8380

Indianapolis Symphony Orchestra
45 Monument Circle
Indianapolis, IN
(317) 639-4300

Minnetrista Cultural Center and Oakhurst Gardens
Muncie, IN
(765) 282-4848

Crown Hill Cemetery
3402 Boulevard Place
Indianapolis, IN
(317) 926-2301

Feast of the Hunter's Moon
Fort Quiatenon Historic Park
Lafayette, IN
(765) 476-8402

Fort Benjamin Harrison U.S. Army Finance Corps Museumt
8000 E. 56th Street
Indianapolis, IN
(317) 542-2169

Benjamin Harrison Memorial Home
1230 N. Delaware Street
Indianapolis, IN
(317) 631-1898

Children's Museum of Indianapolis
3000 N. Meridian Street
Indianapolis, IN
(317) 924-5431

Christ Church Cathedral
125 Monument Circle
Indianapolis, IN
(317) 636-4577

Conner Prairie Pioneer Settlement
13400 Allisonville Road
Noblesville, IN
((317) 776-6000

Indiana State House
100 N. Capitol Avenue
Indianapolis, IN
(317) 232-7615

Indiana Transportation Museum
325 Cicero Road
Noblesville, IN
(317) 773-6000

Indiana World War Museum
431 N. Meridian Street
Indianapolis, IN
(317) 232-7615

Indianapolis Motor Speedway
4790 W. 16th Street
Indianapolis, IN
(317) 241-2500

Hook's Historical Drugstore and Pharmacy Museum
Indiana State Fairgrounds
1180 E. 38th Street
Indianapolis, IN

James Whitcomb Riley Home
528 Lockerbie
Indianapolis, IN
(317) 631-5885

Indiana Basketball Hall of Fame
New Castle, IN
(317) 529-1891

Morris Butler Museum
1204 N. Park
Indianapolis, IN
(317) 636-5409

Indiana Governor's Mansion
4750 N. Meridian Street
Indianapolis, IN
(317) 283-8171

Indiana Medical History Museum
3000 W. Washington Street
Indianapolis, IN
(317) 635-7329

Indiana Museum of Military History
6464 W. 79th Street
Indianapolis, IN
(317) 879-1312

Indiana Soldiers and Sailors Monument
Monument Circle
Indianapolis, IN

Indiana State Museum
650 W. Washington Street
Indianapolis, IN 46204
(317) 232-1637
http://www.in.gov/ism

Madame Walker Theatre
617 Indiana Avenue
Indianapolis, IN
(317) 635-6915

Riley Museum
246 Main Street
Greenfield, IN
(317) 462-8539

Stout Field Military Equipment Museum
1800 S. Holt Road
Indianapolis, IN
(317) 247-3278

Science and Health

Academy of Model Aeronautics National Model Aviation Museum
Muncie, IN
(765) 287-1256

Broad Ripple Planetarium
1115 Broad Ripple Boulevard
Indianapolis, IN
(317) 226-4005

Space Quest Planetarium
The Children's Museum
3000 N. Meridian Street
Indianapolis, IN
(317) 924-4531

Children's Science and Technology Museum of Terre Haute
523 Wabash Avenue
Terre Haute, IN 47807
(812) 235-5548
http://www.terrehaute.com

Cikana State Fish Hatchery
Martinsville, IN
(317) 342-5527

IMAX Theatre
650 W. Washington
Indianapolis, IN
(317) 233-4629

Indianapolis Humane Society
7929 N. Michigan Road
Indianapolis, IN
(317) 876-2415

Indianapolis Water Company
Indianapolis, IN
(317) 639-1501

Indy Parks and Recreation
4649 W. Vermont
Indianapolis, IN
(317) 327-PARK

J. L. Holcomb Observatory and Planetarium
Butler University
Indianapolis, IN
(317) 940-9352

National Weather Service
6900 W. Hanna
Indianapolis, IN
(317) 856-0664

The Flying Pig and Butterfly Ranch
6139 S. County Road 625 W.
Reelsville, IN

White River Gardens
1200 W. Washington
Indianapolis, IN
(317) 630-2001

Parks and Forests

http://www.IN.gov/DNR

Bluesprings Caverns Park
Bedford, IN
(812) 279-9471

Brookville Lake
P.O. Box 100
Brookville, IN 47012 - South Central
(765) 647-2657

Brown County State Park
P.O. Box 608
SR 46
Nashville, IN 47448 - South Central
(812) 988-6406

Cagles Mill/Lieber State Recreation Area
1317 W. Lieber Road
Cloverdale, IN 46120 - Western
(765) 795-4576

Cecil Harden/Raccoon State Recreation Area
160 S. Raccoon Parkway
Rockville, IN 47872 - Western
(765) 344-1412

Chain O'Lakes State Park
2355 E. 75 S.
Albion, IN 46701 - Eastern
(260) 636-2654

Charlestown State Park
SR 62
Charlestown, IN 47111 - Southern
(812) 256-5600

Deam Lake State Recreation Area
1217 Deam Lake Road
Borden, IN 47106 - Southern
(812) 246-5421

Eagle Creek Park and Dam
7840 W. 56th Street
Indianapolis, IN
(317) 327-2461

Ferdinand State Forest
6583 E. SR 264
Ferdinand, IN 47532 - Southern
(812) 367-1524

Garfield Park and Conservatory
2505 Conservatory Drive
Indianapolis, IN
(317) 327-7184

Harmonie State Park
3451 Harmonie State Park Road
New Harmony, IN 47631 - Southern
(812) 682-4281

Harrison/Crawford/Wyandotte Complex
7240 Old Forest Road S.W.
Corydon, IN 47112 - Southern
(812) 738-8232

Indiana Dunes State Park
1600 N. 25 E.
Chesterton, IN 46304 - Northern
(219) 926-1952

Indiana State Fairgrounds RV Campgrounds
1202 E. 38th Street
Indianapolis, IN 46205 - Central
(317) 927-7520
http://www.indianastatefair.com

Lincoln State Park
Highway 162
Lincoln City, IN 47552 - Southern
(812) 937-4710

McCormick's Creek State Park
SR 46
Spencer, IN 47460 - Western
(812) 829-2235

Mississinewa Lake
4673 S. 625 E.
Peru, IN 46970 - Eastern
(765) 473-6528

Monroe Lake
4850 S. SR 446
Bloomington, IN 47401 - South Central
(812) 837-9546

Mounds State Park
4306 Mounds Road
Anderson, IN 46017 - Eastern
(765) 642-6627

Muscatatuck Park
325 N. State Highway 7
North Vernon, IN 47265 - South Central
(812) 346-2953
(800) 928-3667
http://www.muscatatuckpark.com

Ouabache State Park
4930 E. SR 201
Bluffton, IN 46714 - Eastern
(260) 824-0926

Patoka Lake
3084 N. Dillard Road
Birdseye, IN 47513 - Southern
(812) 685-2464

Pokagon State Park
450 Lane 100 Lake James
Angola, IN 46703 - Northern
(260) 833-2012

Potato Creek State Park
25601 SR 4
North Liberty, IN 46554 - Northern
(574) 656-8186

Roush Lake
517 N. Warren Road
Huntington, IN 46750 - Eastern
(260) 468-2165

Salamonie Lake
9214 W. Lost Bridge W.
Andrews, IN 46702 - Eastern
(260) 468-2125

Shades State Park
U.S. 234
Waveland, IN 47989 - Western
(765) 435-2810

Shakamak State Park
6265 W. SR 48
Jasonville, IN 47438 - South Central
(812) 665-2158

Spring Mill State Park
SR 60
Mitchell, IN 47446 - South Central
(812) 849-4129

Squire Boone Caverns and Village
Corydon, Indiana
(812) 732-4381

Summit Lake State Park
5993 N. Messick Road
New Castle, IN 47362 - Eastern
(765) 766-5873

Tippecanoe River State Park
4200 N. US 35
Winamac, IN 46996 - Northern
(574) 946-3213

Tipsaw Recreation Area
248 15th Street
Tell City, IN 47586 - Southern
(812) 547-7051
http://www.perrycountyindiana.org

Turkey Run State Park
SR 47
Marshall, IN 47859 - Western
(765) 597-2635

Versailles State Park
1387 E. US 50
Versailles, IN 47042 - South Central
(812) 689-5606
http://www.camp.IN.gov

Whitewater Memorial State Park
1418 S. SR 101
Liberty, IN 47353 - Eastern
(765) 458-5565

Amusement Park/Water Park

Bearcreek Farms Country Resort
8341 N. 400 E.
Bryant, IN 47326 - Eastern
(260) 997-6822
http://www.bearcreekfarms.com

Deep River Waterpark
9001 E. U.S. Highway 30
Crown Point, IN 46307 - Northern
(219) 947-7850
http://www.deepriverwaterpark.com

Fun Spot Amusement Park
2365 N. 200 W.
Angola, IN 46703 - Northern
(888) 534-8421
http://www.funspotpark.com

Holiday World and Splashin' Safari
Junction of Highways 162 and 245
Santa Claus, IN 47579 - Southern
(877) GOF-AMIL
http://www.holidayworld.com

Indiana Beach Amusement Resort
5224 E. Indiana Beach Road
Monticello, IN 47960 - Western
(574) 583-4141
http://www.Indianabeach.com

Animal Park/Aquarium/Zoo
Black Pine Animal Park
349 W. Albion Road (W. Jefferson Street)
Albion, IN 46701 - Eastern
(260) 636-7383
http://www.blackpineanimalpark.com

Evansville's Mesker Park Zoo and Botanic Garden
2421 Bement Avenue
Evansville, IN 47720 - Southern
(812) 435-6143
http://www.meskerparkzoo.com

Fort Wayne Children's Zoo
3411 Sherman Boulevard
Fort Wayne, IN 46808 - Eastern
(260) 427-6800
http://www.kidszoo.com

Indianapolis Zoo
1200 W. Washington Street
Indianapolis, IN
(317) 630-2001

Inland Aquatics
10 Ohio Street
Terre Haute, IN 47807 - Western
(812) 232-9000
http://www.inlandaquatics.com

ME's Zoo
12441 W. 300 S.
Parker City, IN 47368 - Eastern
(765) 468-8559
http://www.meszoo.com

Pondview Emu Farm
5365 W. Bachelor
Angola, IN 46703 - Northern
(260) 833-9023

Wild Winds Buffalo Preserve
6975 N. Ray Road
Fremont, IN 46737 - Northern
(260) 495-0137
http://www.wildwindsbuffalo.com

Wolf Park
4004 E. 800 N.
Battle Ground, IN 47920 - Western
(765) 567-2265
http://www.wolfpark.org

Performing Arts

Arts Place, Inc.
131 E. Walnut Street
Portland, IN 47371 - Eastern
(260) 726-4809
http://www.artsland.org

Lincoln Amphitheatre
Lincoln State Park
Lincoln City, IN 47552 - Southern
(800) 264-4ABE
http://www.lincoln-amphitheatre.com

PART III

Keys to Indiana Education Law, Standards, and Assessments

"That all citizens will be given an equal start through a sound education is one of the most basic, promised rights of our democracy. Our chronic refusal as a nation to guarantee that right for all children, including poor children, is a national disgrace. We cannot be so blind that we do not see that meeting the most basic needs of so many of our children condemns them to lives and futures of frustration, chronic underachievement, poverty, and violence."

Remarks by U.S. Senator Paul D. Wellstone (MN), Teachers College, Columbia University, March 31, 2000

ACADEMIC STANDARDS

Education is important—so important that simply sending a child to school is not enough. Parents must ensure that their children receive a *quality* education. Regardless of whether children attend a public school, charter school, private school, or home school, there are specific and consistent skills, concepts, and knowledge that children should know on the basis of their grade level. These are referred to as **academic standards**, and they are determined on the state level by the Indiana Department of Education. Parents should know about these standards and be sure that their child's school is meeting them. In addition to the standards and what a child is expected to know, parents need to be aware of Indiana's system for assessing or testing students. These tests are vitally important to the child's future success, and there are ways that parents can help their student perform well. The tests are one of the ways that schools are held accountable for the performance of students, and test scores and data are useful for parents in evaluating overall school performance.

The state of Indiana has established high academic standards for students, and the legislature passed Indiana Public Law 221 to ensure that assessments are administered in a way that improvement is evaluated and individual student performance tracked. The federal No Child Left Behind Act further emphasizes the importance of standards and student assessments and increases federal funding for disadvantaged students in chronically poor-performing schools. This section offers a comprehensive overview of standards, assessments, and accountability and provides the information you need to understand and evaluate the data provided by your school.

Academic Standards

A **standard** is defined as a subject matter benchmark used to measure students' academic achievement. Standards are *open and public statements about what all students should know and be able to do at each grade level.* State standards set consistent goals for the knowledge and skills students should learn in school. Teaching styles and methods may vary, but the educational goals remain constant.

As an example, according to Indiana standards, all Indiana second graders should be able to "use titles, tables of contents, and chapter headings to locate information in text" as a test of reading comprehension. By the eighth grade, students must "evaluate the logic, internal consistency, and structural patterns of text."

Since 1994, all states have been required to adopt challenging academic standards in the core academic areas of mathematics and reading/language arts and make them available to the public. The No Child Left Behind Act requires states to adopt standards in science by 2005–2006.

Indiana's standards have been ranked among the highest in the nation. In its annual "Quality Counts" report, *Education Week* gave Indiana an A- in the area of "standards and accountability." Only eight states received a higher score. Achieve Inc., the Thomas B.

Fordham Foundation, the International Center for Leadership in Education, the American Association for the Advancement of Science–Project 2061, and the National Council for History Education have also ranked Indiana among the best in the country.

You can see how Indiana compares to the rest of the nation by reviewing "The Nation's Report Card," published by **National Center for Education Statistics.** You'll find it at http://nces.ed.gov/nationsreportcard/.

Academic standards are important because:

- Standards promote excellence, fairness, and equality by ensuring that all children are learning the same thing according to grade level regardless of all other factors, such as neighborhood, school, socioeconomic status, race, or gender.
- Standards hold teachers, schools, and school districts accountable for providing children with a quality education.
- Standards enable parents, teachers, and administrators to identify when a child is behind or struggling and to take action, even if the child's grades are sufficient.

Actions for Parents

- Obtain a copy of the academic standards for Indiana. They are available in both English and Spanish at http://www.indianastandardsresources.org and are arranged by subject and grade level.
- Read the standards for your student's grade level thoroughly, asking questions if necessary.
- Look at your child's homework and classwork on a regular basis to see how it matches the standards.
- Visit your child's classroom. Ask the teacher how lessons are aligned with standards.

- Provide feedback to your child's teacher and school, both positive and negative.
- Be involved!

A complete directory of Indiana's state standards can be found at http://www.indianastandards.org.

The Indiana Department of Education also publishes the standards for each subject and grade level in booklet form. Your school may be able to provide the appropriate grade level standards for your child, or you can contact the Indiana Department of Education, Room 229, State House, Indianapolis, IN, 46204-2798.

ASSESSMENTS

Assessment means evaluation, appraisal, or measurement. In Indiana, "assessment" is the word used to describe the academic testing of students. Indiana requires student assessment through the use of annual tests, aligned with the Indiana academic standards, to measure mastery of grade level material presented in the classroom. Annual testing allows teachers, administrators, and parents to obtain more accurate feedback regarding student progress and to take action quickly when needed. Testing is important because it helps schools and teachers plan instruction according to the strengths and needs of their students.

The federal No Child Left Behind Act of 2001 (NCLB) emphasizes the importance of academic standards and requires that all states demonstrate progress toward establishing and meeting standards by requiring annual assessment of students. Under NCLB, by the 2005–2006 school year, all schools will measure student achievement yearly in grades 3 through 8 and at least once during high school. (Currently, most states test once every three to four years.)

NCLB sets up a number of additional requirements:

- States must implement tests in science by 2007–2008.
- States must assess the English proficiency of limited English learners each year.
- Schools must test at least 95 percent of students.

Some important questions to ask about your school district's testing program:

- Do tests students are given match Indiana academic standards?
- Does the school district have a curriculum that is designed to meet and/or exceed state standards?
- Do teachers receive test results in a timely fashion so they can be used to improve instruction and provide help when needed?
- Are test results reported to students, parents, and the community in a timely fashion so they can monitor progress toward meeting standards?
- Are test results reported to parents and students in a way that is easy to understand?

Indiana Statewide Testing for Educational Progress-Plus (ISTEP+) and Core 40 End-of-Course Assessments

Indiana currently uses the **ISTEP+** and **Core 40 End-of-Course** assessments to measure student and school performance. Aligned directly with **Indiana Academic Standards** and what should be taught in the classroom, ISTEP+ is designed to measure students' mastery of Indiana Academic Standards in English/language arts and mathematics through multiple-choice, short-answer, and essay questions, as well as arithmetic problems. The results of the ISTEP+ exam are used to assess individual schools and state and local education programs and to provide a source of educational information for state and local decision makers.

Core 40 End-of-Course assessments will be administered to high school students taking Core 40 classes beginning in 2004. This test measures what students know and are able to do after taking specific courses.

Who takes the ISTEP+ test?

- All students enrolled in **public schools** in Indiana must participate in the ISTEP+.
- Students enrolled in **accredited nonpublic schools** must participate in ISTEP+. If a student has dual enrollment in an accredited nonpublic school and a public school, the student will participate in ISTEP+ testing in the accredited nonpublic school.
- If the student has dual enrollment in a public school and a nonpublic school that is not accredited, the student is a public school student and **must** participate in ISTEP+ testing in the public school. A student who has dual enrollment status is subject to required participation in ISTEP+ testing at the public school unless the student participates in ISTEP+ testing at the nonpublic school.
- If a student is in a local juvenile or adult facility that does not have an educational program, the student will receive educational services from the local school corporation, which includes participation in ISTEP+ testing.
- If the school provides any educational services (alternative education, special education, "last chance" program, etc.) to a student who has been expelled or who faces expulsion, the school must provide ISTEP+ testing to the student.
- A school **may** provide ISTEP+ testing to a student who has been expelled and who receives no other educational services. Some schools have placed conditions on such testing (testing at an alternative site, having a parent or guardian present to ensure good behavior, etc.). If a student is tested through an alternative education program, then the student's scores will be aggregated with the school corporation's results.

Who does not take the ISTEP+ test?

- Students in nonpublic schools that are **not accredited**, including **home schooled students, may not** participate in ISTEP+ testing in their nonpublic school.
- Public schools are not required to provide any services to a student who has been expelled.

What about students with disabilities or limited English proficiency? Accommodations may be available to students with disabilities or limited English proficiency (LEP). Additionally, students who are normally enrolled in a public school but who physically are unable to attend school and who receive current instruction in their homes qualify for ISTEP+ testing under conditions similar to general education students. If such a student requires special testing accommodations, detailed instructions are provided in the *Indiana Statewide Testing for Educational Progress–Plus Program Manual 2004–2005* through the Indiana Department of Education or online at http://www.doe.state.in.us/istep/2004/pdf/progman2004.pdf.

For answers to ISTEP+ questions, call:
ISTEP+ toll-free hotline: (888) 54-ISTEP or (888) 544-7837.

Graduation Qualifying Exam (GQE)

Indiana's GQE is a continuation of the Indiana Statewide Testing for Educational Progress-Plus (ISTEP+) program. Passage of the GQE as a requirement for graduation was passed by the Indiana General Assembly in 1992, part of Public Law 19, in response to concerns of parents, employers, and the higher education community that some graduates were leaving high school without the skills necessary to succeed in the workforce and in post-secondary education.

As a result, Indiana students must demonstrate grade 9 skills in English/language arts, K-8 mathematics, and Algebra I in addition to completing all other state and local graduation requirements in order to be eligible to receive a high school diploma.

New and higher GQE standards were implemented in September 2004. The new GQE guide is available at http://www.doe.state.in.us/istep/2004/pdf/ISTEPNewEra2004.pdf for the Class of 2007.

The GQE is administered over a three-day period in September of a student's grade 10 year.

A student's performance on the test is designated as Pass-Plus, Pass, and Did Not Pass. If a student does not pass all sections of the GQE, he or she may retest in the areas he or she did not pass. Retests are administered in March and are available to juniors, seniors, and adults. No makeup days are offered for the administration of the GQE. **A student has typically has a total of five opportunities to pass the GQE during grades 10 to 12.**

Schools receive money to provide remediation services to all students who do not score above the passing score. Accommodations for students with disabilities or LEP may also be available.

Students can graduate without passing the GQE

State law provides that a student may graduate without passing the GQE if *all* of the following have occurred. The student must have:

- Taken the GQE in the subject area or subject areas in which the student did not achieve a passing score at least one time every school year during his or her sophomore, junior, and senior years in high school;
- Completed remediation opportunities provided by the school;
- Maintained a high school attendance rate of 95 percent, with excused absences not counted against the student's attendance;
- Maintained a C average in the 24 credits required of all Indiana high school graduates (8 in English, 4 in mathematics, 4 in science, 4 in social studies, 2 additional credits in courses already listed or technology competency, 1 in physical education, and 1 in health); and
- Obtained a written recommendation supporting the request for the appeal from the student's teacher(s) in the subject area(s) in which the student has not achieved a passing score and was supported by documentation that the student has attained the academic standard in the subject area based upon tests other than the GQE or classroom work. The principal must approve this recommendation.
- In addition, a student must have satisfied all other state and local graduation requirements.

A student who receives special education services must have the written recommendation of the case conference committee supporting the request for the alternate documentation from his or her teacher of record in consultation with the teacher(s) in the subject area(s) in which the student has not achieved a passing score on the GQE. In addition, the student's case conference committee makes the decision concerning how frequently a student retakes the GQE and how often a student completes remediation (see I.C. 20-10.1-16-13).

Sample GQE test questions are available through the Indiana Department of Education Web site, http://www.doe.state.in.us/istep/pdf/41360_WEB_GQE_Sampler_01IN.pdf.

For more information about the GQE, contact the Indiana Department of Education at (888) 54I-STEP, (888) 544-7837, or go to http://www.doe.state.in.us/istep/welcome.html.

ACCOUNTABILITY

Parents have a right to be informed of data related to academic standards and the results of assessments and to know whether their child, the school, and the school district are progressing toward meeting state standards and how they compare to other schools/districts in the state. **Schools should provide this information willingly and in a manner that is easy to understand.** *Parents also need to be accountable in this process*—taking the time and making the effort to request this information, reviewing the data, providing feedback, and taking action when necessary!

School Report Card

In many states, parents are provided with an accountability report known as a "School Report Card," and this is a requirement under the NCLB Act. Although Indiana does not publish individual school report cards, the information is available on the Web site of the Indiana Department of Education (IDOE) and **Indiana Accountability System for Academic Progress** (ASAP). Created by the IDOE, this Web site helps parents obtain data about school performance and quality. In addition to information about Indiana's academic standards, specific information about Indiana schools is available: for example, how test scores at your child's school compare to state averages.

The ASAP was designed to hold schools responsible for educating Indiana students based on high standards and to challenge them to continuously improve achievement. Beginning with data from the 2002 ISTEP tests, the IDOE will determine whether Indiana school corporations and public schools have met **adequate yearly progress** (AYP) goals under the federal NCLB Act. (See **page 98** for detailed discussion of AYP under the section on NCLB.) Beginning in the 2005–2006 school year, the Indiana State Board of Education will annually place all public schools and those nonpublic schools that voluntarily seek accreditation in a school improvement and performance category based on results from assessments in English and mathematics. AYP under NCLB will be a criterion for category placement.

To find out how an Indiana school or school district is scoring on annual tests, go to http://www.doe.state.in.us/asap/welcome.html.

Indiana Accountability System for Academic Progress:
http://www.doe.in.gov/asap/welcome.html

INDIANA PUBLIC LAW 221

Public Law 221, passed by the Indiana legislature in 1999, created a new system for evaluating school performance. The law directs the principal of each school to develop a three-year "strategic and continuous school improvement and achievement plan" and coordinate an annual review of the plan. The law specifies that the annual review must be made with the input of a committee of persons interested in the school, including administrators, teachers, parents, and community and business leaders appointed by the principal and teachers' organization.

The system mandated by the law measures school success primarily by examining **improvements** in student achievement as measured by ISTEP+. Importantly, the law recognizes that valid measures of improvement must be based on the performance of **the same students** over time.

In order to meet the requirements of the law and determine school improvement on the basis of individual student improvement, a system of unique statewide individual **student test numbers** was put in place in the fall of 2002. Students maintain their individual testing number for all subsequent ISTEP+ administrations.

Indiana already had Public Law 221 in place when the federal government passed accountability measures under NCLB. There are many similarities in the intent of these laws.

For more information, visit http://www.evsc.k12.in.us/curriculum/stand/PubL221.htm.

NO CHILD LEFT BEHIND ACT OF 2001

"No Child Left Behind puts the focus on instruction and methods that have been proven to work. It makes a billion-dollar annual investment to ensure every child learns to read by third grade. And it provides the resources for reform and unprecedented flexibility so states and local communities can get the job done."

—*Rod Paige, Secretary, U.S. Department of Education*

The No Child Left Behind Act of 2001 (NCLB) is a landmark in education reform designed to improve student achievement and change the culture of America's schools. President George W. Bush describes this law as the "cornerstone of my administration." Clearly, our children are our future, and, as President Bush has expressed, "Too many of our neediest children are being left behind."

With passage of NCLB, Congress reauthorized the Elementary and Secondary Education Act (ESEA), the principal federal law affecting education from kindergarten through high school. In amending ESEA, the new law overhauled federal efforts to support elementary and secondary education in the United States.

NCLB is built on four common-sense pillars:

- Accountability for results
- Emphasis on doing what works based on scientific research
- Expanded parental options
- More local control and flexibility

What Does NCLB Mean for Parents and Children?

More information is provided to parents about their child's progress
Under NCLB, each state must measure every public school student's progress in reading and math in each of grades 3 through 8 and at least once during grades 10 through 12. By school year 2007–2008, assessments (or testing) in science will be under way. These assessments must be aligned with state academic content and achievement standards, and results must be provided to parents. This objective data on where their child stands academically helps parents to take action to improve their student's performance.

Parents are alerted to important information on the performance of their child's school
NCLB requires states and school districts to give parents easy-to-read, detailed report cards[26] on schools and districts, telling them which ones are

[26]See information on School Report Cards, page 000.

succeeding and why. Included in the report cards are student achievement data broken out by race, ethnicity, gender, English language proficiency, migrant status, disability status, and low-income status, as well as important information about the professional qualifications of teachers. With these provisions, NCLB ensures that parents have important, timely information about the schools their children attend—whether they are performing well or for *all* children, regardless of their background.

More resource options are provided to children and parents
In this new era of education, children will have more resource options dealing with low-performing schools. Under NCLB, such schools must use their federal funds to make needed improvements. In the event of a school's continued poor performance, parents have options to ensure that their children receive the high-quality education to which they are entitled. That might mean that children can transfer to higher-performing schools in the area or receive supplemental educational services in the community, such as tutoring, after-school programs, or remedial classes.

Improved teaching and learning by providing better information to teachers and principals
Annual tests to measure children's progress provide teachers with independent information about each child's strengths and weaknesses. With this knowledge, teachers can craft lessons to make sure each student meets or exceeds the standards. In addition, principals can use the data to assess exactly how much progress each teacher's students have made and to make better-informed decisions about how to run their schools.

Assurance that teacher quality is a high priority
NCLB defines the qualifications needed by teachers and paraprofessionals who work in any facet of classroom instruction. It requires that states develop plans to achieve the goal that all teachers of core academic subjects be highly qualified by the end of the 2005–2006 school year. States must include in their plans annual, measurable objectives that each local school district and school must meet in moving toward this goal; they must report on their progress in the annual report cards.

Information taken from *No Child Left Behind: A Parents Guide*, available from the U.S. DOE Web site, http://www.ed.gov/parents/academic/involve/nclbguide/parentsguide.html.

Public School Choice

When are children eligible for school choice?
Children are eligible for public school choice when the **Title I school** they attend has not made adequate yearly progress in improving student achievement as defined by the state for two consecutive years or longer and is

identified as "in need of improvement" for corrective action or restructuring. **Any child attending such a school must be offered the option of transferring to a public school in the district, including a public charter school, not identified for school improvement,** unless such an option is prohibited by state law. NCLB requires that priority be given to the lowest-achieving children from low-income families. Starting with the 2002–2003 school year, school choice is available to students enrolled in schools that have been identified as "in need of improvement" under the ESEA as the statute existed prior to the enactment of NCLB.

In addition, children are eligible for school choice when they attend any "**persistently dangerous school**" as defined by the individual state. Any child who has been the victim of a violent crime on the grounds of his or her school is also eligible for school choice.

How do parents know whether their child is eligible for school choice?
Under NCLB, **school districts are required to notify parents** if their child is eligible for school choice because the school has been identified as "in need of improvement" for corrective action or restructuring. The district must notify parents no later than the first day of the school year following the year for which their school has been identified for improvement. States are required to ensure that school choice is offered as an option to parents in the event their child is attending a school that is "persistently dangerous" or if the student has been the victim of a violent crime while on school grounds.

What action can parents take if their school or district does not offer school choice to their child who is eligible?
Schools and districts receiving Title I funds must provide choice for eligible students as described above. If they do not, parents are encouraged to contact the Title 1 office at the Indiana Department of Education.

Do public school options include only schools in the same district?
There may be situations where children in Title I schools have school options outside their own district. For instance, a school district may choose to enter into a cooperative agreement with another district that would allow their students to transfer into the other district's schools. In fact, the law requires that a district try "to the extent practicable" to establish such an agreement in the event that all of its schools have been identified as "in need of improvement" for corrective action or restructuring.

Is transportation available for children who exercise their right to attend another school?
Subject to a funding cap established in the statute, districts must provide transportation for all students who exercise their school choice option under Title I. They must give priority to the lowest-achieving children from low-income families.

Seeking a Quality Education through "Public School Choice"

By Tishika Jackson, M.S. Ed.

In August 2000, my husband and I and our 3-year-old daughter, Jayla, moved to Indianapolis. We were already planning ahead for a school for Jayla to attend, so we made that a priority when choosing a place to live. Our ability to search was limited since we didn't know anyone in Indianapolis to direct us, and we relied on the Internet to find our home. We decided to move to a township school district because it was rumored that your child could receive a better education there than in an inner-city public school.

A year before my daughter began kindergarten, I visited the school that she would attend to register. I was told that she would not be considered for the full-day kindergarten unless there was an "educational need." I didn't understand that. I wanted my daughter to be in an engaging program for a full day to prepare her for "big kid school." But that choice was not offered to me.

My husband and I decided to keep Jayla in day care because they did offer a full-day program. Fearing that she was not receiving everything she needed at school, we purchased home schooling books, workbooks, and educational games. We spent time every day after school making sure she was not being held back.

When Jayla entered first grade, she was evaluated. We were told Jayla was reading at a fourth- to fifth-grade level, and they predicted she would have no trouble in school. My husband and I were relaxed and satisfied. First grade was going to put her right over the top. She was going to be challenged, encouraged, and supported. This is what we thought.

We also wanted to be engaged parents—parents who had a close and constant relationship with Jayla's school and teachers. We joined the PTA, participated in family nights, attended parent/teacher conferences, and did everything we thought was needed to ensure our daughter's success. But within months, we started to notice that her behavior was changing. The work she brought home never seemed to challenge her, and she began getting negative reports from school. We just didn't understand.

When Jayla got her first report card, we were proud—four A's and four B's. She received A's in the core subjects and B's in things like writing and art. At the parent/teacher conference, we asked about accelerated programs to challenge her in reading and language arts skills and math and science. To our dismay, there were no such programs offered at her school. So again, my husband and I were charged with making sure we covered these subjects at home. To our delight, this worked. Our daughter is bright, inquisitive, and brave, but we still fear that she is being held back at her school.

I recently found out through a job interview that my daughter's school has been targeted as "in need of improvement" by the State of Indiana. After all of the effort we put into choosing where to live so she could go to a good school, we still missed something. We felt defeated because we didn't know there were schools designated as "in need of improvement." Drastic changes needed to be made.

We learned that provisions in the No Child Left Behind *legislation allow parents whose children attend schools "in need of improvement" to select another higher-performing public school. We decided the only thing to do was move to an area where the schools were not "in need of improvement." But we wondered, Was that our only option? It's a tough question for us since we live on one income while my husband is a student and we have two children to support. Private school tuition is not an option for us. We also couldn't forget about our youngest child, who had been in the same day care since birth. We feared that moving him would cause a strain on the family. There were almost too many things to consider while keeping up with the daily tasks of life.*

After much thoughtful consideration, we have decided to exercise our right to "public school choice" and have asked that Jayla be transferred to another better-performing school in the district. We are also on the waiting list for a charter school, and we remain hopeful that next year Jayla will have the opportunity to attend a school that can provide a quality education and prepare her for the future.

We have a choice, but it wasn't easy.

One of the provisions of the No Child Left Behind Act *(NCLB) gives the parent of a child attending a school "in need of improvement" the right to choose a better-performing school in the district. My daughter's current school is "in need of improvement," and in last issue of* GEO for Families, *I shared our efforts to choose a better-performing public school for her.* ***I am pleased to say that we were able to choose a new public school, but it wasn't easy.***

After applying for our district's school choice program, we anxiously awaited a reply. We hoped to receive news that my daughter would be in a new school with an environment where most of the children were achieving academic success. One month went by and no word. After the second month, we received a letter from the administration that stated that the school of our choice did not have space for new students and that we would be contacted if there were openings. This was a crushing blow. Again, we had attempted to do what was necessary to find a good school, and again, we had failed.

I immediately called the administration to find out about our status on the waiting list. The associate superintendent told me that my daughter was not "priority" and that her chances of getting into a better-performing school were nonexistent. Tearfully, I asked what my options were, and my questions were met with little regard. Defensively, the associate superintendent said that I had been misinformed about the success of the students at the school and in the administration's opinion, my daughter wasn't in such a bad place. I did not criticize the school or imply that they were not doing their best to serve the children, but I replied that NCLB gives me a right and an option to choose a new school, and that's what I wanted for Jayla. As a mother who works hard to provide the very best for her children, the very best school is what I desire.

Through the professional contacts I have, I was encouraged to pursue my efforts to choose a new school for Jayla. I made a call to the Indiana Department of Education, and they called the associate superintendent on my behalf. The IDOE staff member was told that the school was not budging unless the U.S. Department of Education called and made them!

Finally, after a few more calls, the Title 1 director called and offered an opportunity for Jayla to attend a new public school in my district where most of the children are passing the ISTEP+ tests. I have visited the school and talked with the principal, and I am hopeful that it will meet Jayla's needs and challenge her to achieve her academic potential.

I report this for an important reason. Many parents don't have the support and contacts that I have through the GEO Foundation and would not know what steps to take if the door was slammed in their faces, like it was slammed in mine. I was terribly intimidated by the conversation with the school administration and feared that my daughter would suffer repercussions because of my phone calls—but I had to set that fear aside because failure is not an option.

Tishika Jackson is the director of parent leadership at the GEO Foundation. GEO's mission is to provide information and empowerment for all parents to exercise their rights to choose from a variety of educational options so that all students receive a quality education.

Tips for Parents Who Decide to Stay

In the 2004–2005 school year, nearly 40,000 students who attend the 77 Indiana schools designated by the state as "in need of improvement" are eligible for public school choice. But, if this year is like last year, when the students who transfer are tallied, fewer than 1,000 parents will have transferred their students to higher-performing schools.

There are many reasons why parents may not have chosen to move their student to a new school, but choosing to stay in a school that is "in need of improvement" means that parents need to make an extra effort to be involved with the school and ensure that their children get the education they need and deserve.[27] There are things that parents and caregivers can do to support their children and improve neighborhood schools.

Here are **nine strategies for parents who choose to stay:**

1. **Be a positive influence.** Find out what is going well in the school, and build on it. It is important to point out good work in one area and use it to motivate good work in others.
2. **Ask for extra help for your child.** Often, the local library, YMCA, or other community organizations support schools with after-school programs. Your child may also qualify for free tutoring or other programs through NCLB. See what extra help your school is providing.[28]
3. **Work with your child at home.** Research shows that parent involvement improves student achievement. For suggestions, check out http://www.ed.gov/parents, and ask the school principal or teacher for suggestions about activities you can do at home.
4. **Get involved at the school.** Find out when parents can visit the classroom to observe or volunteer. If it isn't possible for you to visit during school hours, find out what you can do from home to support your child's school.
5. **Make sure your voice is heard at school.** Being a part of the parent organization such as the PTO or PTA offers an opportunity to find out what is currently going on at school and provides a forum to express your opinion.

---

[27]"Choosing Better Schools: a Report on Student Transfers under the No Child Left Behind Act." Report of the Citizen's Commission on Civil Rights. May 2004. Cynthia G Brown, Principal and Investigator.

[28]The GEO Foundation maintains a list of free and low-cost tutoring services available in central Indiana.

6. **Evaluate the school's improvement plan.** Does it focus on areas where the school is not doing well? Do all classes offer high-quality teaching and a challenging curriculum so that all children will meet the standards? What areas have been identified as needing improvement? Ask how you can help.
7. **Get a copy of the parent involvement policy from the principal, parent liaison, or head of your school's parent group.** Under No Child Left Behind, parents have a right to participate as a member of the school's improvement team. Parents should be involved in *meaningful* ways in making decisions about the academic programs and policies. Ask to be a member of these committees.
8. **Talk with other parents.** What do they think about the school's parent involvement policy? Does it cover their concerns? Talking with other parents strengthens the school community and builds support and awareness. There is strength in numbers, and parents are more powerful when they work together.
9. **Review the school-parent compact.** Was it developed with and approved by parents? Every school is supposed to have a compact, which is an agreement between the school and the parent. Make sure the compact outlines how the school will provide a supportive and effective learning environment for all students.

Supplemental Educational Services

What are supplemental educational services?
Supplemental educational services, such as tutoring or other after-school programs, are designed to increase the academic achievement of students in schools that have not met Indiana targets for increasing student achievement for three or more years. These services are to be provided in addition to the regular school day by a different provider than the school. Services for students may be offered through public- or private-sector providers approved by the state, such as public schools, public charter schools, local education agencies, educational service agencies, and faith-based organizations. Private-sector providers may be either nonprofit or for-profit entities.

Indiana maintains a list of approved providers across the state organized by the school district or districts they serve from which parents may select. You can find this information online at the **State-Approved Supplemental Services Provider List,** http://www.doe.state.in.us/esea/ses-0405/.

When are children eligible to receive supplemental educational services?
Students from low-income families who stay in Title I schools that fail to meet state standards for at least three years are eligible to receive supplemental educational services.

Are parents notified about supplemental educational services?
Yes. Local schools are *required* to provide annual notice to the parents of eligible children about the availability of services and information on the approved providers.

Can parents choose providers for tutoring and other supplemental educational services?
Yes, parents of eligible children can choose from the list of state-approved providers. Indiana has approved a diverse list of providers. Upon request, the school will help parents determine which provider would best fit their child's needs. When parents have made their selection, the school must then contract with that provider to deliver the services.

What action can parents take if their child is eligible for tutoring or other supplemental educational services but their school or district does not offer them?
Districts receiving Title I funds *must* offer free tutoring and other extra help to eligible students. If eligible students are not being offered these services, parents are encouraged to contact the Title 1 office at the IDOE, 151 West Ohio Street, Indianapolis, IN 46204, or call toll free (877) 418-7240 or fax (317) 233-6502.

How are providers of supplemental educational services held accountable?
The federal government required Indiana to develop and apply objective criteria for evaluating and monitoring the quality of services that that providers offer. In addition, supplemental services providers must give to parents, as well as to the school, information on their children's progress.

Adequate Yearly Progress (AYP)

Adequate yearly progress (AYP) is a signaling system indicating whether schools are on track to teach students what they need to know. Each state sets its own and the same goals for all schools and students. The goals gradually increase over time. **The ultimate goal is that all students will meet the state's standards for "proficiency" in reading and math by 2014.** AYP is the formula for determining whether schools are meeting these goals.

There are two ways for a school to meet AYP requirements:

- If a school's actual achievement is at or above the state goal in a given year, the school is designated as making AYP.
- The AYP formula also gives credit to low-performing schools that have made significant progress. If a school or group of students within a school does not meet the goals but the number of students below proficiency level is reduced by 10 percent from the year before, the school still makes AYP. This is known as the "**safe harbor**" provision of NCLB.

Schools "in need of improvement"
If a school **has not made AYP for two years in a row,** it is designated as "**in need of improvement,**" and a number of sanctions apply. A school does not meet AYP if either (1) the entire school or (2) a specific group of students within the school does not meet state standards.

Indiana and AYP
Indiana's standards for assessing AYP are based primarily on the percentage of students passing ISTEP+ each fall. Indiana has set the following goals in order to ensure that 100 percent of students are proficient in reading and math by 2014. (See http://www.doe.state.in.us/esea/pdf/Accountability081403.pdf.)

Fall Testing	English/Language Arts	Math
2002, 2003, 2004	58.8%	57.1%
2005, 2006, 2007	65.7%	64.3%
2008, 2008, 2010	72.6%	71.5%
2011	79.5%	78.7%
2012	86.4%	85.9%
2013	93.3%	93.1%
2014	100%	100%

Indiana Schools "in Need of Improvement"

The list of **Indiana schools "in need of improvement"** was released by the Indiana Department of Education on July 29, 2004—just three weeks before the start of the 2004–2005 school year. Of the 438 schools, **77 are listed as Title I schools** "in need of improvement" according to the provisions of the No Child Left Behind Act.

To see whether the school your student attends is "in need of improvement," see the GEO Foundation Web site, http://www.geofoundation.org, or http://www.doe.state.in.us/esea/welcome.html.

Corrective Action Timeline for Title I Schools in Need of Improvement
After failing to make AYP for two years, the following timeline is in effect:

Year One: Public School Choice
Parents must be notified of the status of their school and of their school choice options. Students can transfer to a different school in the district that

is not in need of improvement, and the district is responsible for covering transportation costs.

Year Two: School Choice and Free Tutoring (SES)
Students can exercise school choice. As an alternative, the school must notify parents of eligible students and supply them with free tutoring services. Tutoring services are free to the student. The school pays the independent service provider for tutoring.

Year Three: School Choice, Free Tutoring, and Corrective Action
In the third year, the district must identify the school for corrective action, and parents must be notified. Corrective action must include at least one of the following:

- Replace school staff
- Institute new curriculum
- Decrease management authority
- Appoint an outside expert to advise the school
- Extend the school year/day
- Restructure the school's organizational structure

Years Four and Five: School Choice, Free Tutoring, Corrective Action, and Alternative Governance
If a school remains on the "in need of improvement" list for a fourth year, a plan for alternative governance must be developed and implemented in the fifth year. Alternative governance includes closing and reopening as a charter school, turning management of the school over to a private corporation, or establishing a community-based management team.

INDIANA EDUCATION LAW: FREQUENTLY ASKED QUESTIONS

When is a child required to be in school?
Children must be enrolled in school during the school year the child turns age 7 for public school and age 7 for nonaccredited, nonpublic school (Sec.IC.20-8.1-3-17 (b) and (h)). The starting age for kindergarten does not affect the starting age for first grade. The Indiana Code does not have an age for eligibility for first grade, just for school attendance.

Must a student have a birth certificate to enroll?
No, any reliable source of proof is accepted. A child may not be denied enrollment due to a lack of documentation.

May a school withhold records from a requesting school because a student did not pay book fees or other school fees?
No. The statute says a school "shall" release the records upon request. School records are official documents and do not "belong" to public schools. Indiana Code 20-8.1-9-10 specifically prohibits withholding benefits and privileges of education from a public school child due to a parent's failure to pay required fees.

May a school refuse to enroll a child between the ages of 7 and 18 who has not been suspended or expelled if the child lives in the school corporation area?
No. If a child is presented for enrollment after the beginning of school, the child must be enrolled. Children must be in school when the school is in session. Failure to be in school when the school is in session may be truancy. Some schools have set a 10- or 15-day limit, and if a child comes to school after that limit, the school refuses to enroll that child. This policy violates the Compulsory School Attendance Law and may not be legally enforced.

May a school deny enrollment to a student over the age of 18? How does a public school decide legal settlement or discipline for students over the age of 18?
Students over the age of 18 are not required to attend school under the Compulsory School Attendance Law, but they have the right to an education under the Constitution of the State of Indiana, Article 8, Section 1. The policy of the Department of Education is that students who have not graduated (earned a diploma) from high school are eligible for attendance in public schools.

Must the parents have documentation to prove their residence?
No. Parents must enroll their child within the boundaries of the school corporation in which they (the parents) live. If documentation is unavailable, the school must enroll the child and then verify residence by a school official or attendance officer home visit.

May schools use the custodial agreement forms, prepared by the Indiana Department of Education and approved by the Superintendent of Public Instruction, in cases where a person other than a parent wants to enroll a child?
Yes. Persons other than the parent may be caring for the child, and the custodial agreement forms are to be used. If the school believes that a student does not legally reside within the school corporation boundaries, the student (after enrollment) may be expelled following due process of law.

What are the laws governing home education?
The Compulsory School Attendance Law governs the education of all children, in all schools, up to the age of 18. For more information, ask for the brochure *The Relationship of Public Schools and Home Schools*, available from the State Attendance Officer, by calling (317) 232-9132.

Do home educators have to provide curricula, an educational plan, or other proof of educational services to the public schools to show that they are competent to educate in their home?
No. The only records home educators must furnish, when requested by the local or state superintendent, are attendance records. Issues of equivalency or neglect are questions that should be referred to the proper authorities, which may include Child Protection Services, the Prosecutor's Office, or law enforcement.

Who has the responsibility for a child's attendance in school?
(a) The student (see LC.20-8.1-3-17)
(b) The parent (see LC.20-8.1-3-33)
(c) The school corporation administrator and the administrator of any educational, correctional, charitable, benevolent institution, or training school having children under the institution's authority (see LC.20-8.1-3-36)

When may a child withdraw for child labor reasons?
Students must be at least 14 years of age to secure a work permit. It is unlawful for any person, firm, limited liability company, or corporation to hire, employ, or permit any child less than age 14 to work in any gainful occupation (LC.208.1-4-1 and LC.20-8.1-4-3). Work permits are obtained at the local high school. (See **page 000**, "Working and High School.")

May students be placed in community service as a disciplinary action?
Yes, students may be required to perform community service activities, up to 120 hours, with parent permission (LC.20.1-5.1-18).

What disputes may be heard by the Indiana State Board of Education?
(a) All appeals from an order expelling a child under LC.20-8.1-5.1-11
(b) All appeals provided for in LC.20-8.l-6.1

(c) All disputes regarding:
- Legal settlement
- Right to transfer right to attend school in any school corporation
- Amount of transfer tuition
- Any other matter arising under this chapter

What rights do parents have?

(a) The **right to send their children to school** in the corporation in which they live.

(b) The **right to have the child attend the school** that the child attended at the completion of the child's eleventh grade, without regard to the parent's change of address.

(c) The **right to appeal** to the State Board of Education on questions of rights to attend school, legal settlement, transfer tuition, and other matters.

(d) The **right to examine their child's educational records** in accordance with the Family Educational Rights and Privacy Act.

(e) The **right to be informed of a student's suspension** from school.

(f) The **right to be informed of a meeting to expel** their child.

(g) The **right to withdraw their child** from public school **subject to the child receiving an education equivalent** to the public school.

(h) The **right to free, appropriate education** of a child with suspected disabilities under the Individuals with Disabilities Education Act (IDEA) and the Administrative Rules of the Indiana State Board of Education.

(i) The **right to request an evaluation** of a child with suspected disabilities.

(j) The **right to question information in a school record** and place a statement in that record describing facts that the parents believe are misleading or inaccurate (see subparagraph 12.d and Administrative Rules of the Indiana State Board of Education, 511 IAC 7-8-1 (n)).

For more information regarding Indiana law, contact:

Indiana Department of Education

State Attendance Office

(800) 833-2199

http://www.doe.state.in.us

HOW TO ADVOCATE FOR YOUR CHILD

Everywhere we turn, parents are encouraged to be more responsible for their children's education. Most educators would agree that at the very least, this means sending children to school ready to learn, with a good night's rest and a nutritious breakfast. Being responsible for our children's education also means advocating for them when a problem occurs at school.

Whether it's a bully on the playground or poor classroom performance, parents can be more effective when they have a strategy. It's important not to let emotions come into play. Here are 10 simple steps to follow when a problem arises at school:

1. **Define and examine your concerns.** Do your homework. To be believable, it is critical to collect all the facts and articulate the problem clearly. Does this problem involve other children? If so, consider involving other parents in this process. There is credibility in numbers.
2. **Develop possible solutions.** This sets a positive tone indicating you want to work in partnership with the school to resolve the problem. You are not merely complaining but offering potential solutions.
3. **Prepare a written document.** To an extent, the education system has forced school personnel into the role of bureaucrats, and their language is paper. Having a written document makes the school take your concerns seriously. The document should contain a list of your issues, potential solutions, and questions. The tone should reflect your desire to work positively with the school.
4. **Meet with the teacher.** Make an appointment with the teacher. Consider having your spouse or a friend accompany you for support. Inform the teacher who to expect at the meeting.
5. **Approach the meeting with a positive attitude.** Leave your emotions outside the meeting room. Negative behavior will only discredit your message; your behavior must stay above reproach. Using your document as the basis for the meeting's agenda, keep an open mind, and don't be afraid to ask questions.
6. **Define the next step.** At the end of the meeting, ask:
   - What is the next step?
   - Who will be responsible for that step?
   - When (date) will the next step occur?

   This step is crucial; it keeps the meeting from being merely a gripe session and increases the likelihood of a positive outcome. Leave a copy of your written document with the teacher.

7. **Document events.** Keep a record of all meetings and phone calls, including dates and people involved along with *your* initial document and any letters. Politely informing the school that you are documenting the events lets the school know *you* are serious.
8. **Follow the chain of command.** If *you* and the teacher are unable to resolve the problem, go to the next link in the chain of command. Usually the chain of command looks like this: teacher, principal, superintendent, school board member. *Use* steps 1 through 7 with each person on the chain.
9. **Consider all your educational options.** If your child's school is unwilling to work with *you* to resolve the problem, look at the other educational choices parents have in Indiana. Parents now have more *free* choices than ever before, including public charter schools, limited private school vouchers, or other district schools. The GEO Foundation can help you learn more about your options.
10. **Never forget: you are responsible for the education of your children.** You are the only constant from kindergarten through college in *your* children's education. There is no guarantee that any educational system will ensure *your* children's educational needs are met; ultimately, it's *your* responsibility. Don't abdicate that responsibility to *your* children's schools; delegate and oversee it. Your children's futures depend on it.[29]

[29]Reprinted with permission from the August 2001 issue of ***Parent Power***, published by **the Center for Education Reform** in Washington, D.C., a nonprofit organization founded in 1993 to provide support and guidance to parents, teachers, and those who are working to bring fundamental reforms to their schools. Phone: (800) 521-2118; Web site: http://www.edreform.com.

KEYS TO RECORD KEEPING:
Which Documents Are Keepers?

Record Keeping for Parents

If you've got kids in school, you can be overwhelmed by the paperwork in no time at all. From the time a child enters school until the time he or she graduates, the accumulation of evaluations, progress reports, correspondence, notes, journals, samples of your child's work, and medical records will fill several drawers of a file cabinet or take up most of your shelf space.

You might be tempted to throw out papers when they get out of hand, but this may be a mistake. Even the oldest documents in your child's history can sometimes help you make a case for increased or different services at your school.

Make sure you understand the relative importance of different documents and organize them sensibly.

Which Documents Are Keepers?

Here's a list of the different documents that you'll see over the course of your child's education. You should keep them all!

1. **Evaluations by the school system and by independent evaluators.** Depending on your child, these will include educational, psychological and/or neuropsychological, speech and language, occupational therapy, and physical therapy evaluations.
2. **Medical records.** Keep records of your child's immunizations and any pertinent health information. If the school provides vision, hearing, or scoliosis reports or recommendations, keep them. Any other communication from the school regarding communicable diseases, etc., should be kept. As with any other kind of document, when in doubt, keep it!
3. **Progress reports and report cards.** These are the formal documents where the school system periodically describes how your child is doing.
4. **Standardized test results.** School systems often administer standardized tests (such as the ISTEP+ or GQE) to all students. These tests can provide a helpful comparison to the progress reports written by your child's teachers.
5. **Notes on your child's behavior or progress.** These will include notes from you to the teacher, from the teacher to you, or journal entries. Sometimes notes from a concerned teacher tell a different story than the formal report the teacher develops at the request of the school administration.

6. **Correspondence.** Save any correspondence between you and teachers or the school. Don't forget e-mails—print them out and include them in your correspondence file. Also save correspondence from the school system that's addressed to you or to all parents describing issues that affect your child. This may include letters describing new programs, changes in programs or services, school system policies, or budget issues.
7. **Notes from conversations and meetings** with school personnel, evaluators, or other interactions relating to your child. If you are called to the school for an important meeting, take excellent notes, or, better yet, bring someone with you whose only task is to take notes. These notes can help enormously when, months later, you try to remember exactly what various people said or what agreements were reached.
8. **Documents relating to discipline and/or behavioral concerns.** These include notices of detention and suspension (both in and out of school), letters describing the concerns of service providers or school administrators about behavior, records of behavioral assessments, and records of behavioral plans for addressing behavioral issues.
9. **Formal notices of meetings scheduled to discuss your child.** When you get a notice, jot down the date you received it. Sometimes the question of whether a school system has met time requirements is important.
10. **Samples of schoolwork.** You don't need to keep every scrap of writing or drawing that your child produces, but it can be helpful to keep examples each year. You can compare these to show how much progress has been made in different academic areas.
11. **Invoices and cancelled checks.** Save receipts for book rentals, lunches, or other school-related expenses.
12. **Public documents.** These include school newsletters and newspaper articles featuring administrators, school committee members, or superintendents talking about school policy, programs, cutting expenses, new teaching approaches, etc.

Your Child's School Records

Visit the school office every once in a while to look at your child's student records. You want to be sure that you have all the documents the school has. Find out whether you have documents that the school doesn't. You can also find out about the rules and regulations in your state for accessing your child's records. In general, all states must provide access under a federal law called the Buckley Amendment (the **Family Educational Rights and Privacy Act of 1974**, 20 U.S.C. §§ 1221, 1232g).

Typically, you have the right to see the records, wherever they are kept, and to have copies provided to you. You may also have the right to ask that a certain document be removed. If your request is denied, you can appeal the decision.

What Documents Should You Create?

Why is it important to create documents? One reason is that you may have to tell your child's story to another person—an evaluator, an advocate or lawyer, or a hearing officer—in order to get help, especially in the case of special education students. Documenting events as they occur will help you tell the story accurately. A second reason is that documents can help clarify understandings you reach with people, particularly with service providers or school administrators. A third reason is that documents that are written when something happens support you when you need to prove that the event happened the way you say it happened.

Keep a Journal

It can take years for parents to realize that they should have kept better notes of meetings, telephone calls, and important events in their child's educational career. If your young child has a disability in need of special education, get ahead of the game by developing this habit now.

Your notes may be important later when you need an accurate description of what key people said at a meeting, at a parent meeting, or in an evaluator's office.

Some parents keep a journal with dates, short descriptions of events or conversations, and the names of people who were involved. This doesn't mean you need to include every tiny detail of your child's life, but a well-kept journal can help you explain to others (or to yourself) how you got to the current situation.

Try to record these events:

- Dates of meetings with school personnel
- Dates you received key documents
- Dates you sent or delivered key documents
- Dates you gave school personnel important information (such as "1/7/99: Told Mary's teacher that she'd been spending three hours every night trying to do 15-minute math assignments")
- Dates on which your child was suspended or disciplined

Create Agreements

Some documents are designed to record understandings reached with others. The most formal example of this is a contract signed by the parties who agree to its terms. An individualized educational plan (IEP) is really a contract. It records an agreement reached between parents and school systems that govern (1) the types of services to be delivered to a child for a specific period of time, (2) the location of those services, and (3) the identity of service providers. Each party signs it.

Even without an "official" agreement, you can create your own document to help prove that an understanding was reached. Here's an example:

Your special education director tells you that the school system will hire an expert on inclusion techniques. You'll be given the chance to meet with the expert about your child. Follow up this conversation with a friendly letter to the director. In the letter, thank her for taking the time to discuss your concerns about the classroom, and describe your understanding of the steps she promised to take. End your letter by asking the director to respond immediately if you have misunderstood anything.

This letter may not "prove" that the director said what you claim she said, but if she doesn't send back a response, there's an implication that she did say those things.

Other Documents

There may be other documents that can help your child. Has your child been tested repeatedly over the years, with steadily declining results? Have the people who work with your behaviorally involved child wondered what precipitates aggressive outbursts? Keep a record of the things that are said and done, whether witnessed by you or told to you. You may be able to solve the mystery and focus your child's teachers on developing a plan to work with these behaviors.

Finally

Keep your children's records in a file box or other safe place. These permanent records will be invaluable to you if your child has special needs or displays behavior problems at the school. Remember, you are your child's best advocate, and you are the expert. Having the documents to back up your opinion will give you added confidence in working with the school.[30]

Student Privacy Rights

Schools keep records of your child's academic and personal progress, from kindergarten through graduation. And some schools keep student files for many years after the child has graduated or left. Student records can include quantitative information like test scores, intelligence quotients (IQs), and grades. **They also can include more subjective information** like progress

[30]This article was adapted from ***The Paper Chase: Managing Your Child's Documents under the IDEA*** by Robert K. Crabtree, Esq. http://www.fetaweb.com/03/paperchase.crabtree.htm.

reports, psychological and psychiatric reports, and teacher evaluations. The only time a school is allowed to release student records without getting a parent's permission is in emergency situations where the information is necessary to protect your health and safety or those of other students.

For more information see *Your Right to Keep Your School Records Private*, American Civil Liberties Union, July 17, 2003, http://www.aclu.org/StudentsRights/StudentsRights.cfm?ID=13152&c=161.

PART IV

Key Family Matters

- Healthy Families
  - Health Education
  - Immunizations
  - Communicable Diseases
  - Health Screenings
  - Nutrition
    - National School Lunch Program
- Addictions
  - Drugs
  - Alcohol
  - Tobacco
- Violence
  - Prevention
  - School Safety
  - Domestic Violence
- Pregnancy
- Fathering
- Housing
- Employment
- Emergency Services
- Runaways

THEO
NIKO
A CROW
1 M
2 F V
3 Mt

HEALTHY FAMILIES

"Schools could do more than perhaps any other single institution in society to help young people, and the adults they will become, to live healthier, longer, more satisfying, and more productive lives."

—Carnegie Council on Adolescent Development

There is a growing recognition that children's health directly affects their ability to learn and achieve academically. It is difficult for children to be successful if they are tired, hungry, stressed, using drugs or alcohol, or being abused. Schools are addressing these issues in a variety of ways, including health education, physical education, and nutrition. This is an area where parents can get involved, making sure that schools are offering a safe and healthy environment, opportunities for physical activity, and nutritious meals in the cafeteria.

Why Is Health Education Important?

It is a sad fact that:

- One in seven students has been in a physical fight on school property
- Every 60 seconds, a child is born to a teen mother
- Obesity affects one in five children in the United States
- Each day, 3,000 children start smoking—one every 30 seconds
- One in three high school students reports having consumed five or more drinks in a row
- Every four hours, a child in America commits suicide

Indiana Philosophy and Rationale for the Health Education

Health education is essential to the health and learning of children and adolescents. The health and health-related behaviors of students have a direct impact on their school attendance and ability to learn. Health education in schools is also essential because many health behaviors are initiated during childhood and are related to many of the leading and preventable causes of disease, disability, and death in the United States. Researchers indicate that health education in schools represents an effective way to enable students to develop the knowledge and skills that they need to avoid health risks and enhance both their health and their academic achievement. Health education provides students with the knowledge and skills they need to enhance not only their personal health but also the health of their families, schools, and communities.

The **Indiana Administrative Code** recommends weekly minimum time allocations for health education such as:

- Grades 1, 2, and 3: motor skills development and health education (105 minutes weekly)
- Grades 4, 5, and 6: health and safety education (75 minutes weekly)
- Grades 6, 7, and 8: health and safety education (100 minutes weekly)
- High school graduation requirement: 1 credit

A school corporation that currently is operating with less than the minimum minutes recommended for health education may find it necessary to increase the minutes allocated for health education in order to fully meet the standards for health education as outlined in the Indiana standards for health education.[31]

The Future: Coordinated School Health Program (CSHP)

The IDOE's **Coordinated School Health Program** (CSHP) office, in collaboration with the American Cancer Society Great Lakes' Region and the Michigan Department of Education, has selected 10 school corporations to participate in a three-year intensive leadership-training program from Indiana and Michigan. CSHP concentrates on the well-being of K-12 students and not only focuses on the collaboration of health and physical education but also includes other components needed to help schools become healthy and productive. These other components address food service, health services, counseling, psychological and social services, staff wellness, and family and community support. This excellent program offers great promise as a tool for schools to promote wellness among students and families and hopefully will be expanded to include all Indiana school corporations.

For more information on this new program, see http://www.doe.state.in.us/cshp/components.html.

Immunizations Are Important

It's important for children to be vaccinated—or get their "shots"—so they don't get childhood diseases. Your child can be vaccinated at the doctor's office or your local health department. Ask the doctor to give you a list of the shots your child has received, and keep the list so that you have records for school and so you'll know whether your child needs more shots.

Vaccines are available today to protect your child against:

- diphtheria
- whooping cough (pertussis)
- tetanus

[31]http://www.doe.state.in.us/standards/Docs-Health/HealthIntro120202.doc

- polio
- measles
- mumps
- German measles (rubella)
- Chicken pox (varicella)
- hepatitis B
- HIB (haemophilus influenzae type B)
- pneumococcal diseases

Required Immunizations

In Indiana, state law (Indiana Code IC 20-8.1-7-9.5) requires that all children be immunized against **diphtheria, pertussis (whooping cough), tetanus, measles, rubella, poliomyelitis, and mumps.** In addition, every child who enters kindergarten or grade 1 must be immunized against **hepatitis B.**

The first shots for most of these illnesses should be given when the child is still a baby. This is important because most of the diseases these vaccines protect your child against can be serious or even deadly.

Like any medicine, vaccines carry a small risk of serious harm such as a severe allergic reaction. But side effects from shots are usually mild and last only a short time. Some children have no side effects at all. None of the possible side effects should keep your child from getting shots unless your doctor says so.

Be sure to tell your doctor if anyone in your immediate family has ever had a bad reaction to a vaccine, and ask whether there are certain conditions under which vaccination is not recommended. Also talk to your doctor about whether certain reactions to vaccines can be controlled, such as by giving your child acetaminophen before or after vaccination.

Immunizations required for school enrollment in Indiana:

Indiana Code IC 20-8.1-7-10.1 states that schools shall require parents of a child who has enrolled in the school to furnish no later than the first day of school a written statement of the child's immunizations, accompanied by physician's certificates or other documentation. In some cases, parents may receive a waiver based on a child's prior health history or religious objections.

For more information:

Department of Health and Human Services, Food and Drug Administration
5600 Fishers Lane (HFI-40)
Rockville, MD 20857
http://www.fda.gov/opacom/lowlit/shots.html

Schools and Communicable Disease

Indiana Code 20-8.1-7-8 states the following in regard to children with communicable disease and the school:

> IC 20-8.1-7-8 Children found to be ill; treatment; readmission; determination of local health officer; appeals.

Sec. 8 (a) If a child is ill, has a communicable disease, or is infested with parasites, the school principal may send the child home with a note to the child's parent or guardian. The note must describe the nature of the illness or infestation and, if appropriate, recommend that the family physician be consulted.

(b) If the parent or guardian of a child who is sent home under this section is financially unable to provide the necessary medical care, it shall be provided by a public health facility. If no public health facility is available, the township trustee or other appropriate governmental agency shall provide the necessary relief.

(c) A child who is sent home under this section may be readmitted to the school:

(1) when it is apparent to school officials that the child is no longer ill, no longer has a communicable disease, or is no longer infested with parasites;
(2) upon certification of a physician that the child is no longer ill, no longer has a communicable disease, or is no longer infested with parasites;
(3) upon certification by a physician that the child has a communicable disease but the disease is not transmissible through normal school contacts; or
(4) upon certification by a Christian Science practitioner, who is listed in the Christian Science Journal, that based on the practitioner's observation, the child apparently is no longer ill, no longer has a communicable disease, or no longer is infested with parasites.

If school personnel disagree with the certifying physician or Christian Science practitioner as to whether the child should be readmitted to school, the local health officer shall determine whether the child may be readmitted to school.

(d) A person who objects to the determination made by the local health officer under this section may appeal to the secretary of the Indiana State Department of Health, who is the ultimate authority. IC 4-21.5 applies to appeals under this subsection. (Formerly: Acts 1973, P.L. 218, Sec. 1.) As amended by P.L. 196-1987, Sec. 4.

Quick Reference Chart: Common Communicable Diseases in School-Age Children

Disease	Incubation Period	Communicability	Exclusion Laws
Campylobacter Enteritis	From 1-10 days; usually 1-7 days	Throughout acute infection and as long as organisms are in stool.	Yes
Chickenpox (Varicella)	From 10-21 days; usually 14-16 days	As long as 5 days, but usually 48 hours before onset of rash, or until all vesicles have scabbed.	Yes
Conjunctivitis (Pink Eye)	Bacterial: 24-72 hours; Viral: usually 12 hours-3 days	Dependent upon cause of the infection.	Yes
Cryptosporidiosis	From 2-14 days; average 7 days	Throughout acute infection and as long as organisms are in stool.	Yes
E. Coli 0157:H7	From 2-8 days; usually 3-4days	Throughout acute infection and as long as organisms are in stool.	Yes
Fifth Disease	From 4-14 days; up to 6 days	During acute stage of illness.	No*
Hand, Foot, and Mouth Disease	Usually 3-6 days; up to 6 days	During acute stage of illness.	No
Hepatitis A	From 15-50 days; average 25-30 days	Greatest risk is in 2 weeks preceding onset of jaundice; risk is minimal after one week following jaundice onset.	Yes
Measles	From 7–18 days; average 10 days	1–2 days before beginning of prodromal period to 4 days after rash appears.	Yes
Mononucleosis	4–7 weeks after exposure	Indeterminate.	No
Pediculosis (Lice)	Eggs hatch in 1 week; lice can multiply in 8–10 days; lives 20–30 days	As long as live lice remain on an infested person, or until eggs are 1/4" away from scalp.	No
Ringworm	From 4–10 days	As long as infection is present.	No**
Salmonellosis	From 6 hours–3 days; usually 12–36 hours	Throughout acute infection and as long as organisms are in stool.	Yes
Scabies	From 2–6 weeks	During duration of illness.	Yes
Shigellosis	From 1–7 days; usually 2–4 days	Throughout acute infection and as long as organisms are in stool.	Yes
Strep Throat	Usually 1–3 days	Usually 24–48 hours if under treatment.	No

* (may exclude if fever present)

** (exclude from some activities)

IC 16-41-9-3
Sec. 3.

(a) The local health officer may exclude from school a student who has a dangerous communicable disease that:

(1) is transmissible through normal school contacts; and
(2) poses a substantial threat to the health and safety of the school community.

(b) If the local health officer subsequently determines that a student who has been excluded from school under subsection (a) does not have a dangerous communicable disease that:

(1) is transmissible through normal school contacts; and
(2) poses a substantial threat to the health and safety of the school community; the local health officer shall issue a certificate of health to admit or readmit the student to school.

(c) A person who objects to the determination made by the local health officer under this section may appeal to the executive board of the state department, which is the ultimate authority. IC 4-21.5 applies to proceedings under this section.

Hearing, Vision, and Scoliosis (Posture) Screenings

Under Indiana law, school corporations are required to conduct tests of vision, hearing, and posture (IC 20 –8.1-7-16, IC 20 –8.1-7-17, IC 20 –8.1-7-19).

Vision tests are to be conducted upon enrollment in kindergarten or first grade, annually for students in the third and eighth grades, and of all students suspected of having a visual defect. The school is required to make and maintain records of these screenings in order to provide information useful in protecting, promoting, and maintaining the health of school children.

Schools are required to conduct **hearing screenings**, or tests, in the first, fourth, seventh, and tenth grades of all transferred school children and all children suspected of having hearing defects.

These screenings allow schools to identify students who may not be taught well in a regular classroom and to make appropriate alternative plans for remedial or correctional devices. In every case, the school is required to advise the child's parents of the proper medical care, attention, or treatment that is needed.

Scoliosis
A test to determine postural defects shall be administered to each public school student in grades 5, 7, and 9.

Nutrition

Home-cooked, nutritious meals, healthy appetites, family mealtimes—it sounds ideal, but it's not always easy, not in a society filled with working parents, microwaves, and fast-food restaurants on every corner. Although it will not add hours to your day or make your kids like broccoli, this information will help you keep your children—and yourself—healthy and happy!

Habits for a Healthy Life

- **Eat the right foods.** Use the daily serving suggestions below as much as possible.
- **Eat the right amounts.** Serve your child portions that fit the three A's: age, appetite, and activity. Be sure your child gets enough milk, and limit fats and sweets! It is also important to monitor the number of calories your children consume. Most children require 2,200 calories, with more active children requiring more and less active children requiring fewer. Recent studies suggest that 10 percent of all elementary school students are overweight.
- **Exercise daily.** Make exercise a fun family activity: bike, walk, swim, play ball, fly a kite!

Food Groups: Daily Servings for a Healthy Diet

Dairy: 2–3 servings
The dairy group includes milk, cheese, ice cream, and yogurt. These foods are important for calcium, which is needed for strong bones and teeth.
1 serving = 1 cup of milk or yogurt or 1–1 1/2 oz. natural cheese or 2 oz. processed cheese

Protein: 2–3 servings
The protein group is made up of meats, poultry, fish, beans, and nuts. These foods contain protein, zinc, and iron.
1 serving = 2–3 oz. of cooked lean meat, poultry, fish or 1/2 cup cooked dry beans or 1 egg or 2 tablespoons of peanut butter or 1/2 cup nuts

Vegetables: 3–5 servings
The vegetable group contains carrots, broccoli, cauliflower, potatoes, and other vegetables. Vegetables are good sources of vitamins, minerals, and fiber.
1 serving = 1 cup raw leafy vegetables or 1/2 cup other vegetables or 3/4 cup vegetable juice

Fruits: 2–4 servings
The fruit group includes strawberries, apples, bananas, oranges, and other fruits. Fruits provide vitamins, minerals, and fiber.
1 serving = 1 medium apple, banana, orange, etc., or 1/2 cup canned fruit or 3/4 cup fruit juice

Grains: 6–11 servings
The grains group contains foods such as bread, rice, cereal, and pasta. Grains are important for vitamins, minerals, complex carbohydrates, and dietary fiber.
1 serving = 1 slice of bread or 1 oz. cereal or 1/2 cup rice or pasta

Resources for healthy eating at home and school:
Brown Bag Success: Making Healthy Lunches Your Kids Won't Trade by Sandra K. Nissenberg and Barbara N. Pearl
The authors of this book have created both a cookbook and a nutritional guide for parents.

Secrets to Feeding a Healthy Family by Ellyn Satter
This book discusses ways to plan healthy meals for children and adults.

http://www.actionforhealthykids.org
This is a nationwide initiative involving education and health leaders. In Indiana, contact
Clarion Health Promotions, (317) 962-9017, for a brochure entitled "Mom, I'm Hungry: What to Feed Your Hungry Children."

http://www.nutritionforkids.com
This Web site offers a free "feeding kids" newsletter and a recipe index.

National School Lunch Program (NSLP)

The NSLP is a federally assisted meal program operating in more than 99,800 public and nonprofit private schools and residential child care institutions. It provides nutritionally balanced low-cost or free lunches to more than 26 million children each school day. The program was established under the National School Lunch Act, signed by President Harry Truman in 1946.

In 1998, Congress expanded the National School Lunch Program to include reimbursement for snacks served to children in after-school educational and enrichment programs to include children through 18 years of age.

What are the nutritional requirements for school lunches?
School lunches must meet the applicable recommendations of the Dietary Guidelines for Americans, which recommend that no more than 30 percent of an individual's calories come from fat and less than 10 percent from saturated fat. Regulations also establish a standard for school lunches to provide one-third of the recommended dietary allowances of protein, vitamin A, vitamin C, iron, calcium, and calories. School lunches must meet federal nutrition requirements, but local school food authorities make decisions about what specific foods to serve and how they are prepared.

How do children qualify for free and reduced-price lunches?
Any child at a participating school may purchase a meal through the NSLP. Children from families with incomes at or below 130 percent of the poverty level are eligible for free meals. Those with incomes between 130 percent and 185 percent of the poverty level are eligible for reduced-price meals, for which students can be charged no more than 40 cents. (For the period July 1, 2003, through June 30, 2004, 130 percent of the poverty level is $23,920 for a family of four; 185 percent is $34,040.)

Children from families with incomes over 185 percent of poverty pay full price, though their meals are still subsidized to some extent. Local school food authorities set their own prices for full-price (paid) meals but must operate their meal services as nonprofit programs. After-school snacks are provided to children on the same income eligibility basis as school meals. However, programs that operate in areas where at least 50 percent of students are eligible for free or reduced-price meals serve all snacks free of charge.

For more information:
United States Department of Agriculture http://www.fns.usda.gov/cnd/Lunch/AboutLunch/NSLPFactSheet.htm
IDOE: Division of School and Community Nutrition Programs
http://www.doe.state.in.us/food, (317) 232-0855, or
http://www.doe.state.in.us/food/schoolnutrition/welcome.html

An Apple a Day Can't Keep the Junk Food away from the School Cafeteria

There's something wrong when salsa passes as a vegetable in the school cafeteria and students can buy candy and soda from vending machines on campus. Read on to learn why your child's health may be endangered by what he or she eats at school.
By Lisa Rosenthal, GreatSchools.net Staff

Remember when the U.S. Department of Agriculture (USDA) declared ketchup a vegetable in 1986 and caused a huge uproar? Although ketchup eventually lost its vegetable designation, the USDA now sanctions commercially prepared salsa as a vegetable. The condiment figures prominently on school cafeteria menus, along with pepperoni pizza, submarine sandwiches, and french fries.

Disturbing Statistics
Schools across the country, where 53 million children eat lunch every day, face a dilemma: what to serve that will be nutritionally sound yet appealing to young people. Schools are supposed to abide by the federal government's nutritional standards in order to receive reimbursements, but many schools are forfeiting federal dollars by selling out to fast-food franchises, which share

profits with schools and appeal to children's tastes by providing such lunch items as burgers, fries, and pizza.

Alarming statistics about children's health are being revealed almost daily:

- *In the past 25 years, the percentage of overweight children ages 6 to 11 has nearly doubled from 7 percent to 13 percent.*
- *U.S. spending on hospital costs related to childhood obesity has tripled in the past two decades.*
- *Type II (adult-onset) diabetes, which used to affect mostly adults, is now appearing at an increasing rate in children.*
- *Obesity across all age levels has reached epidemic levels. According to a recent Surgeon General's report, half of all Americans are overweight. Obesity is associated with hypertension, gall bladder disease, and diabetes.*

The Allure of Candy and Soda

Fat-laden offerings in school cafeterias are not the only problem. In this era of declining school budgets, schools are supplementing their incomes by allowing candy and soda machines on campuses. Overall, vending machine sales nationwide account for $750 million annually in extra money for schools. One school district in Arizona expects to gain $2.2 million over five years from soda and candy sales.

These sales aggravate the child health problem. A study by Children's Hospital in Boston shows that drinking one can of soda a day increases a child's risk of obesity by about 50 percent. To add fuel to the fire, children are bombarded with advertisements for soda, fast foods, and sugar-coated cereals when they watch television.

Ironically, at the same time that children are sipping Cokes and eating Milky Ways, more and more schools are being forced to trim physical education programs due to budget cuts and the increased emphasis on academics in order to prepare students for standardized tests. The combination of decreased physical activity with poor eating habits is contributing to the increase in childhood obesity, experts say. William Potts-Dalema of the Harvard School of Public Health says there is a "clear and compelling link" between physical education and nutrition programs and improved academic performance. He believes schools can make a difference by beefing up these programs.

Bucking the Trends

The news is not all gloom and doom. Some state legislatures are taking action, and individual school districts are starting to "just say no" to soda and candy. For example:

- *After protests by parents, students, and school officials, more than 30 school districts in California, Tennessee, and Wisconsin have refused to sign contracts with soft drink vendors.*
- *The state legislature in California recently passed a law banning the sale of junk food in elementary schools and the sale of soda in elementary and middle schools. (The law says nothing about sales of these products in high schools.)*
- *In Texas, sales of soft drinks, candy, and other products of low nutritional value near school cafeterias are illegal.*

Grow It, Cook It, Eat It

If students learn where their food comes from or participate in growing and cooking it, they are more likely to make healthy food choices. That's the belief of famed restaurateur and cookbook writer Alice Waters. Her California restaurant, Chez Panisse, started a national trend when it opened in 1971 and focused on fresh, locally grown organic fruits and vegetables.

In an effort to take her message to the schools, Waters contracted with the Berkeley School District in 2001 to run part of its food service. That program didn't quite meet its goals in terms of organic food sales, but it did heighten awareness around healthy eating.

Other innovative programs that support healthy nutrition in schools include:

- ***The Garden in Every School Initiative**, a California Department of Education program that provides free information packets to schools and funds garden-enhanced nutrition with mini-grants to schools.*
- ***Team Nutrition**, a USDA program that provides schools with nutrition education materials and showcases healthy changes in school meals and innovative nutritional education programs.*
- ***Kids Café**, a project with 600 locations nationwide, mostly in schools and Boys and Girls Clubs, whose purpose is to teach kids about healthy eating while providing them with free healthy snacks, such as smoothies, that they learn to make themselves.*
- ***The Healthy Schools Summit**, the first-ever meeting bringing together top educators, doctors, and nutritionists to draw attention to the topic of children's health. Chaired by former U.S. Surgeon General David Satcher with first lady Laura Bush as honorary chair, it is sponsored in part by the National Dairy Council. It took place October 7–8, 2002, in Washington, D.C.*
- ***The Growing Roots Project** in Arizona, which is dedicated to helping students connect to the earth through scientific investigation and creative expression. The organization sponsors field trips in Arizona and offers teacher training, assemblies, and curriculum assistance.*

What Can Parents Do?
Here are some tips, based in part on recommendations from the American Dietetic Association, on how you can improve your child's nutrition at school and at home:

- ***Get familiar with the menu.*** *Keep a current school lunch menu, and discuss it with your child. Talk about making healthy choices.*
- ***Get involved.*** *Join or start a parent advisory council for the school food service program.*
- ***Support the nutrition education efforts at school.*** *If your school has an edible garden, volunteer to help. If none exists, create one. Support school lessons about nutrition with healthy eating at home.*
- ***Encourage your child to pack his or her own lunch.*** *Help him or her pick healthy choices that are fun to eat, such as string cheese, fruit, carrot sticks, and pudding cups. If your child packs it, he or she will be more likely to eat it.*
- ***Advocate for stronger laws.*** *Write to your representatives at the state and federal level. Express your concerns about the nutritional quality of school lunches, the placement of vending machines on school campuses, and budget cuts affecting physical education programs.*

Reprinted with permission from the Greatschools.net Web site, http://www.greatschools.net.

ADDICTIONS

A report entitled *Malignant Neglect: Substance Abuse and America's Schools*, published in September 2001 by the National Center on Addiction and Substance Abuse at Columbia University, states:

> For at least 9.5 million high school students (60 percent) and almost five million middle school students (30 percent), back to school means returning to places where illegal drugs are used, kept, and sold. For six consecutive years, 12- to 17-year-olds have reported that drugs are the number one problem they face. Each year substance abuse costs our schools at least $41 billion dollars in truancy, special education, and disciplinary programs, disruption, teacher turnover, and property damage ...[32]

Drug abuse is costly to our society as a whole but is especially harmful to our youth. Their immature physical and psychological development makes them more susceptible than adults to the harmful effects of drug abuse. Behavior patterns that result from teen and preteen drug use often produce tragic consequences. Self-degradation, loss of control, disruptive conduct, and antisocial attitudes can cause untold harm to juveniles and their families.

The study *Malignant Neglect* is 126 pages and can be downloaded for free from the CASA Web site, http://www.casacolumbia.org/pdshopprov/files/80624.pdf. The report is the first comprehensive analysis of all available data on substance use in our schools and among our students. It is designed to clarify how tobacco, alcohol, and illicit drug use affect schools and to suggest what it will take to make our schools and children substance free. The following paragraphs have been reprinted in the hope that parents will want to read the entire report.

"Many caring individuals have wrestled with the problem of drugs in our schools, but perhaps the report's most troubling indictment is that the infestation of our schools with alcohol and drugs is due to malignant neglect of parent, teachers, administrators, communities, and the students themselves.

"Parents raise hell and refuse to send their kids to classrooms infested with asbestos or lice. Yet every day they ship their children off to schools riddled with illegal drugs ...

"Teachers hold parents accountable ... Administrators look to zero-tolerance policies and brief curriculum courses ... Parents blame the schools and teachers ... Teachers blame the parents. School administrators point to lack of community support ... Students blame peer pressure and lack of parent interest ...

---

[32]CASA. *Malignant Neglect: Substance Abuse and America's Schools*. Columbia University. 2001. http://www.casacolumbia.org/pdshopprov/files/80624.pdf.

"The finger pointing and denial constitute a conspiracy of silence that threatens millions of our nation's children and savages many of them for life ..."[33] (p. ii)

Some CASA Key Findings

- By the time students complete high school, 70 percent (11.1 million) have smoked cigarettes, 81 percent (12.8 million) have drunk alcohol, 47 percent (7.4 million) have used marijuana, and 24 percent (3.8 million) have used another illicit drug. Each year, there are 13.2 million incidents where a 12- to 17-year-old tries tobacco, alcohol, marijuana, ecstasy, or some other illicit drug.
- Relatively few students who experiment with a substance discontinue its use. Among students who have ever tried cigarettes, 85.7 percent (2.1 million) are still smoking in the twelfth grade. Of those who have ever been drunk, 83.3 percent (2.1 million) are still getting drunk in the twelfth grade. Of those who have ever tried marijuana, 76.4 percent (1.4 million) are still using it in the twelfth grade.
- Zero-tolerance policies and drug testing in schools may help identify students in trouble but often are used merely to identify children for expulsion.[34]

What can be done?

"There are no silver bullets to keep schools and students substance free, and schools alone cannot be expected to solve the problem.

"Parents bear primary responsibility for keeping their children drug free. School administrators, as well as teachers, bear the primary responsibility for keeping drugs, alcohol, and nicotine off their grounds. Students bear a responsibility to help keep themselves, their friends, and their schools drug free. Communities and governments have responsibility to keep the streets and neighborhoods drug free and to provide an environment in which children can grow up substance free. In this sense, all of the above are responsible for the fact that millions of our high school and middle school children are sent every day to schools where drugs are used, kept, and sold."[35]

The CASA report includes suggestions for schools, communities, and parents. For the purpose of this publication, we are including just the opportunities for parents.

---

[33]CASA. *Malignant Neglect: Substance Abuse and America's Schools*. Columbia University. 2001. http://www.casacolumbia.org/pdshopprov/files/80624.pdf, p. ii.

[34]CASA. *Malignant Neglect: Substance Abuse and America's Schools*. Columbia University. 2001. http://www.casacolumbia.org/pdshopprov/files/80624.pdf, p. 2.

[35]CASA. *Malignant Neglect: Substance Abuse and America's Schools*. Columbia University. 2001. http://www.casacolumbia.org/pdshopprov/files/80624.pdf, p. 6.

Opportunities for Parents

Parents should become "hands-on" parents by, for example:

- Eating dinner with their children on most nights of the week—with the television off.
- Making clear that they would be extremely upset if their children smoked, drank, or used drugs.
- Expecting to be and are told the truth by their children about where they are going in the evenings or on weekends.
- Knowing where their children are after school and on weekends.
- Imposing a curfew.
- Being very aware of their children's academic performance.
- Monitoring what their children watch on television and do on the Internet.
- Putting restrictions on the music CDs their children buy.
- Having children be responsible for regular household chores.
- Having an adult present when their children are home from school.
- Fighting for substance-free schools.[36]

Drug Abuse

In the seven years that the National Center on Addiction and Substance Abuse (CASA) at Columbia University has published the *National Survey of American Attitudes on Substance Abuse*, results have indicated that teens and their parents view drugs as their biggest concern.

Indiana law requires that every school corporation establish a Drug-Free Schools Committee, consisting of school personnel, parents, and community representatives. **As a parent, you can get involved by serving on your school's drug-free committee.**

Should Schools Test Children for Illegal Drugs?

It is an important question and one that must be decided by parents, teachers, and school administrators. A decision in June 2002 by the U.S. Supreme Court expands the authority of public schools to test for drugs, but it is still up to individual communities and schools to decide whether drugs are a significant problem and testing is appropriate. The Office of National Drug Control Policy has put together a booklet entitled *What You Need to Know about Drug Testing in Schools*. It can be a helpful resource for parents who want to know more about this issue.

See **Drug Testing in Schools**, http://www.doe.state.in.us/sdfsc/pdf/DrugTestingONDCP.pdf.

---

[36]CASA. *Malignant Neglect: Substance Abuse and America's Schools*. Columbia University. 2001. http://www.casacolumbia.org/pdshopprov/files/80624.pdf, p. 9.

Indiana Law Regarding Addiction Instruction

IC 20-10.1-4-9.1 Alcoholic beverages, tobacco, prescription drugs, and controlled substances; instruction in kindergarten through grade 12

Sec. 9.1. (a) Beginning in the 1991–1992 school year, the governing body of each school corporation shall for each grade from kindergarten through grade 12 provide instruction concerning the effects that alcoholic beverages, tobacco, prescription drugs, and controlled substances have on the human body and society at large.

(b) The board shall make available to all school corporations a list of appropriate available instructional material on the matters described in subsection (a).

(c) The department shall develop curriculum guides to assist teachers assigned to teach the material described in subsection (a).

(d) The board shall approve drug education curricula for every grade from kindergarten through grade 12.

(e) The department shall provide assistance to each school corporation to train at least one (1) teacher in the school corporation in drug education.

As added by P.L.342-1989(ss), SEC.15. Amended by P.L.51-1990, SEC.16.

IC 20-10.1-4-9.2 Drug-free schools committee; composition; duties

Sec. 9.2. (a) To facilitate the establishment of drug-free schools in Indiana, the governing body of each school corporation shall establish a drug-free schools committee for each school in the school corporation.

(b) Each committee must consist of not more than fifteen (15) members who represent the following from the school corporation:

(1) School personnel.
(2) Parents of students.
(3) Representatives of the community.

(c) Appointments to the committee shall be made in compliance with contractual provisions, discussion procedures, or past practice.

(d) Each committee shall do the following:

(1) Develop a drug-free school plan that:
    (A) requires each school to collect and report drug-related activities in the school, including suspensions, expulsions, exclusions, police actions, or any other type of drug-related behavior; and (B) addresses ways to eliminate illegal drugs and drug-related behavior in schools.
(2) Oversee the implementation of the school plan.
(3) Oversee the implementation of the curriculum under section 9.1 of this chapter.

As added by P.L.51-1990, SEC.17.

More information:
The U.S. Department of Education, Office of Preventing Drug Use among Children and Adolescents: *A Research-Based Guide for Parents, Educators, and Community Leaders*, Second Edition, http://165.112.78.61/Prevention/prevopen.html.

How to Tell Whether Your Child May Be in Trouble with Alcohol[37]

The **National Council on Alcoholism and Drug Dependence Inc.** (NCADD) provides the following common indicators that suggest your child may be involved with alcohol and in need of help and guidance.

- Smell of alcohol on breath or sudden, frequent use of breath mints.
- Abrupt changes in mood or attitude.
- Sudden decline in attendance or performance at school.
- Losing interest in school, sports, or other activities that used to be important.
- Sudden resistance to discipline at school.
- Uncharacteristic withdrawal from family, friends, or interests.
- Heightened secrecy about actions or possessions.
- Associating with a new group of friends whom your child refuses to discuss.

Numerous community organizations can help parents and students prevent and confront involvement with alcohol and other addictive substances. Don't wait to get help!

Alcoholics Anonymous (AA)
(888) 4AL-ANON, (888) 425-2666
http://www.alanon.com/
Alcoholics Anonymous is a national organization in operation for more than 50 years helping individuals, family, and friends with the family disease alcoholism. The disease affects family, friends, school, and work. Most communities in the United States host AA meetings where a 12-step program is applied for both Al-Anon adult and Alateen youth sessions.

Greater Indianapolis Council on Alcoholism and Drug Dependence
2511 East 46th Street, Building M
Indianapolis IN 46205
(317) 542-7128
E-mail: indianapolis.in@ncadd.org
This program is affiliated with the National Council on Alcoholism and Drug Dependence Inc. (NCADD). Visit http://www.ncadd.org.

---

[37] *How to Tell If Your Child May Be in Trouble with Alcohol.* December 1, 2004. The National Council on Alcohol and Drug Dependence Inc. http://www.ncadd.org/facts/parent2.html.

Hope line: (800) NCA-CALL (24-hour affiliate referral)
These organizations fight the stigma and the disease of alcoholism and other drug addictions. Programs and services include advocacy, awareness, intervention, prevention, and treatment. The site has an extensive fact section that includes information for youths and adults.

Fairbanks
8102 Clearvista Parkway
Indianapolis, IN 46256-4698
(317) 849-8222
http://www.fairbankscd.org
Fairbanks is a nonprofit addictions treatment center. Their Web site contains information on facing addictions and research articles about addictions.

Narcotics Anonymous (NA)
http://www.narcoticsanonymous.org/
http://www.naindiana.org/
Narcotics Anonymous (NA) is an international, community-based association of recovering drug addicts seeking fellowship and support facing their addiction. The organization began in the 1940s as an off-shoot from Alcoholics Anonymous. Meetings are regularly held across Indiana. Log onto the Indiana Web site at http://www.naindiana.org/ for meeting listings in your community.

Family and Social Services Administration
http://www.in.gov/fssa/
The **Family and Social Services Administration** helps people with mental illness and gambling or chemical addictions who are uninsured or underinsured to receive treatment and reintegrate into the community. Fees for services are based upon income level. FSSA's Division of Mental Health and Addiction operates six state hospitals and partners with Indiana's Community Mental Health Centers to provide treatment in communities across Indiana. For a list of additional counseling providers in Indiana, visit http://www.in.gov/fssa/.

Indiana Prevention Resource Center
Indiana University, Creative Arts Building
2735 E. 10th Street, Room 110
Bloomington, IN 47408-2602
(812) 855-1237
Toll free in Indiana: (800) 346-3077
Fax: (812) 855-4940
http://www.drugs.indiana.edu

This center is Indiana's primary source for alcohol-, tobacco-, and other drug-prevention resources.

The Importance of Family Dinners
September 2003
The National Center on Addiction and Substance Abuse at Columbia University
This report presents the findings of CASA's Family Day survey. The survey of 1,987 teens ages 12 to 17 found that the number of teens who have regular family dinners drops by 50 percent as their substance abuse risk increases sevenfold. The survey demonstrates the importance of regular family dinners, finding that compared to teens who have family dinners twice a week or less, teens who have dinner with their families five or more nights in a week are 32 percent more likely never to have tried cigarettes (86 percent vs. 65 percent), 45 percent likelier never to have tried alcohol (68 percent vs. 47 percent), and 24 percent likelier never to have smoked pot (88 percent vs. 71 percent). This report also includes survey findings on the relationship between family dinners and teens' academic performance. Based on research showing that frequent family dinners reduce the risk of teens smoking, drinking, and using illegal drugs, CASA first promoted "Family Day: A Day to Eat Dinner with Your Children" in 2001. Since then, "Family Day" has been gaining acceptance and has been endorsed by numerous states, cities, counties, government agencies, community groups, and private companies.

You can download a free copy of this report at http://www.casacolumbia.org/pdshopprov/files/Family_Dinners_9_03_03.pdf.

VIOLENCE PREVENTION

Violence and crime can affect anyone at anytime, and anyone can act to prevent violence and crime. Parents need to teach children that violence is not the way to solve problems and that there are better ways to resolve conflict. It's easy to avoid the issue of violence, but it's too important to ignore, and parents are the ones who have the most influence over young children. Children can learn to control anger and resolve conflict, and they learn the most by watching the adults in their lives.

Below are some suggestions on how to prevent violence in your family and community:

- **Know where and how to report potentially violent situations or concerns.** Ask your local police department for help in identifying what to report, when, to whom, and how.
- **Support schools and youth clubs in their efforts to keep guns, knives, and other weapons away from children and teens.** Encourage children to report weapons they know about to a trusted adult.
- **Look around to see what opportunities are available for kids and teens during after-school hours!** If no programs are available, take action! Talk to your child's school, churches, etc. (See SAVE, described below.)
- **Take steps to protect yourself and your family at home.** Invest in effective locks, a dog, or an alarm system.
- **If you choose to own firearms, make sure they are safely stored in a locked place with ammunition separately locked.**
- **Show children how to settle arguments or solve problems without using words—or actions—that hurt others.** It's okay for your child to witness conflict; this is a chance for you to **teach him or her how to solve conflicts nonviolently!**
- **Take a good look at what you, your family, and your friends watch and listen to for entertainment.** Talk to your children about these things!

National Association of Students against Violence Everywhere (SAVE)
http://www.nationalsave.org/
322 Chapanoke Road, Suite 110, Raleigh, NC 27603
Toll free: **(866) 343-SAVE** Local: **(919) 661-7800**
SAVE is a student-driven organization. Students learn about alternatives to violence and practice what they learn through school and community service projects. As they participate in **SAVE** activities, students learn crime prevention and conflict-management skills and the virtues of good citizenship, civility, and nonviolence. SAVE chapters can be started in elementary schools, high schools, and community organizations. SAVE will be happy to mail you a free introductory packet that includes sample activities, pledges, and crime prevention and conflict-management information, as well as information on service projects.

Currently, these Indiana schools have SAVE chapters: Brunswick Elementary School, Gary; Edgewood Junior High, Ellettsville; Muncie Central High School, Muncie; North High School, Evansville; Reitz High School, Evansville

School Safety

The Indiana Department of Education **Indiana School Safety Specialist Academy** Web site, http://www.doe.state.in.us/isssa, offers current information on school safety and violence prevention issues, such as crisis response for parents, war and terrorism, bullying, suicide prevention, video game violence, and hate crimes. The site includes excellent materials and links.

11 Tips to Help Parents Create Safer Schools[38]

1. **Take an active role in your child's school.**
2. **Find out what is already being done at your child's school.** Try to learn about the school's overall approach to safety and security. If you are not sure, ask the principal to provide more information.
3. **If your child's school has a school safety committee, ask to join.** If not, organize one. Visit http://www.ncpc.org/besafe for ideas.
4. **Make it clear to your student that you support school policies and rules** that help create and sustain a safe place for all students to learn.
5. **Listen to and talk with your child about problems or concerns.** Bullying, fistfights, and shoving are safety issues at many schools.
6. **Help your child learn how to solve conflicts peacefully.**
7. **Make sure your child knows that you won't tolerate violent behavior.** Discourage name-calling and teasing, which often become more violent.
8. **Insist on knowing your child's friends, whereabouts, and activities.** *It's your right as a parent!*
9. **Work with other parents to develop standards** for behavior both in and out of school. Support other parents, and require adult supervision.
10. **Play it safe.** If you choose to keep guns in the home, make sure they are securely locked and that children know weapons are never to be touched without permission and supervision. You are responsible for your child's actions with your gun.

---

[38] *11 Tips to Help Parents Create Safer Schools*. KSA Plus Communications. http://www.ksaplus.com.

11. **Know your rights.** The federal No Child Left Behind Law allows students in persistently dangerous schools to transfer to a safer school.

For more information regarding school safety programs, resources, and related Web sites, visit http://www.doe.state.in.us/isssa/newresources.html.

Domestic Violence

Children are "highly sensitive recording devices" able to recognize and remember everything that goes on around them—including violence. No matter how hard you try to hide domestic violence from your children, they know. And as a result, children become victims as well. Domestic violence is often much more traumatic for children than adults, even if they do not directly witness violence. Adults are fully developed individuals who are able to meet their own basic needs physically, socially, and emotionally. Children, however, rely on adults—usually their parents—to provide these needs. If children are not provided with a safe environment and trustworthy caretakers, they can develop harmful symptoms that will affect them throughout their life. Some of these include:

- General fearfulness.
- Difficulty concentrating.
- Hyper-vigilance: the child is always on-guard, waiting for something bad to happen.
- Nightmares.
- Various troubled responses to fear, anger, and sadness; this can include not displaying these emotions at all.
- Fear of being separated from or losing a parent.
- Quickly formed attachments to adults they do not know.
- Confusion about parental loyalties: whose side should the child be on?
- Ambivalence about abusive parent: children love the abusive parent but at the same time fear and feel anger toward him or her.
- Feelings of powerlessness: children are unable to leave an abusive situation. Children often develop defensive responses. It's better to be the abuser than to be abused.
- Sense of guilt and responsibility for being unable to protect the abused parent.
- Difficulty resolving conflicts and aggressive behavior.

Children learn so much from parents. If they witness violence in the home, they not only learn to hit, kick, bite, and push when they're angry, but they also begin to see these behaviors as "normal." Girls who witness domestic violence while growing up are much more likely to be in abusive relationships as adults, and boys are much more likely to be abusers. This is what they know; this is what they were taught by the people they love and admire the most—their parents.

If you or someone you know is involved in a violent relationship, there is help available.

Indiana Coalition against Domestic Violence (ICADV)
1915 W. 18th Street
Indianapolis, IN 46202
(317) 917-3685
Toll free: (800) 538-3393
Crisis line: (800) 332-7385
http://www.violenceresource.org
The Indiana Coalition against Domestic Violence Inc. (ICADV) recognizes domestic violence as a physically and psychologically damaging cultural, social, and a criminal problem and is committed to its elimination. ICADV recognizes that violence occurs in all relationships, that everyone is affected by it, and that the solution involves everyone. This statewide organization provides information on programs and referrals to women in need of domestic violence shelter statewide. The Web site includes information regarding the Indiana statutes regarding domestic violence and defines battery.

ICADV Hotline
(800) 332-7385 Voice and TTY
The Indiana Coalition Against Domestic Violence Inc. operates the statewide 24-hour toll-free hotline for victims of domestic violence in partnership with Alternatives Inc. of Madison County. Individuals calling the crisis line receive emotional and practical support that includes but is not limited to the following: crisis counseling, criminal justice information, personal advocacy, information and referral services, and violent crime compensation assistance. The hotline has TTY capabilities as well as Spanish-speaking advocates to assist callers.

Alternatives to Domestic Violence (Family Services)
615 N. Alabama, Suite 320
Indianapolis, IN
(317) 634-6341 (ext. 185 for Spanish-speaking clients)
http://www.family-service-inc.org
This program is a 26-week group for men, women, and children whose lives have been affected by domestic violence. Perpetrators must acknowledge violence. Treatment focuses on the cycle of violence, safety planning, conflict resolution, stress management, and improving communication skills. It is free for women and children and is priced on a sliding scale for men. (Medicaid and most private insurances are accepted.) It serves Boone, Hancock, and Marion Counties.

Legal Assistance
Protective Order Pro Bono Project
(317) 638-7672
http://www.popbp.org
This project offers free assistance to victims of domestic violence trying to obtain and/or enforce protective orders. It provides an attorney and law student to represent the victim.

PREGNANCY

The United States has the highest rates of teen pregnancy and births in the Western industrialized world. Teen pregnancy costs the United States at least $7 billion annually. Thirty-four percent of young women become pregnant at least once before they reach the age of 20—about 820,000 a year. Eight in 10 of these pregnancies are unintended, and 79 percent are to unmarried teens.[39]

In 1999, there were 11,301 births by mothers 19 years old or younger in Indiana.[40]

Teen Pregnancy Consequences

Teen mothers are less likely to complete high school (only one-third receive a high school diploma), and only 1.5 percent have a college degree by age 30. Teen mothers are more likely to end up on welfare (nearly 80 percent of unmarried teen mothers end up on welfare).

The children of teenage mothers have lower birth weights, are more likely to perform poorly in school, and are at greater risk of abuse and neglect.

The sons of teen mothers are 13 percent more likely to end up in prison, while teen daughters are 22 percent more likely to become teen mothers themselves.

Teen Pregnancy Prevention

The primary reason that teenage girls who have never had intercourse give for abstaining from sex is that having sex would be against their religious or moral values. Other reasons cited include desire to avoid pregnancy, fear of contracting a sexually transmitted disease (STD), and not having met the appropriate partner. Three of four girls and more than half of boys report that girls who have sex do so because their boyfriends want them to.

Teenagers who have strong emotional attachments to their parents are much less likely to become sexually active at an early age.

Most people say teens should remain abstinent but should have access to contraception. Ninety-four percent of adults in the United States and 91 percent of teenagers think it's important that school-aged children and teenagers be given a strong message from society that they should abstain from sex until they are out of high school. Seventy-eight percent of adults also think that sexually active teenagers should have access to contraception.

---

[39] *Teen Pregnancy Statistics and Prevention.* http://www.familyfirstaid.org/teen-pregnancy.html. 1/04/05.

[40] Indiana State Department of Health. *Births and Age-Specific Rates by Race and Age of Mother*: Indiana, 1999.

Contraceptive use among sexually active teens has increased but remains inconsistent. Three-quarters of teens use some method of contraception (usually a condom) the first time they have sex. A sexually active teen who does not use contraception has a 90 percent chance of pregnancy within one year.

Parents rate high among many teens as trustworthy and preferred information sources on birth control. One in two teens say they "trust" their parents most for reliable and complete information about birth control; only 12 percent say a friend.

Teens who have been raised by both parents (biological or adoptive) from birth have lower probabilities of having sex than teens who grew up in any other family situation. At age 16, 22 percent of girls from intact families and 44 percent of other girls have had sex at least once. Similarly, teens from intact, two-parent families are less likely to give birth in their teens than girls from other family backgrounds.[41]

This information was obtained from the *FamilyFirstAid* Web site, http://www.familyfirstaid.org.

Indiana Law Regarding Instruction on Human Sexuality

IC 20-10.1-4-11

Instruction on human sexuality or sexually transmitted diseases

Sec. 11. Throughout instruction on human sexuality or sexually transmitted diseases, an accredited school shall:

(1) teach abstinence from sexual activity outside of marriage as the expected standard for all school-age children;

(2) include that abstinence from sexual activity is the only certain way to avoid out-of-wedlock pregnancy, sexually transmitted diseases, and other associated health problems; and

(3) include that the best way to avoid sexually transmitted diseases and other associated health problems is to establish a mutually faithful monogamous relationship in the context of marriage.

As added by P.L.134-1988, SEC.3.

[41] *Teen Pregnancy Statistics and Prevention.* http://www.familyfirstaid.org/teen-pregnancy.html. 1/04/05.

Additional Help and Information

Crisis Pregnancy Center
(800) 395-HELP (4357)
http://www.cpclink.com
The center provides crisis pregnancy counseling, pregnancy prevention information, and resources.

Medline Plus, a service of the U.S. National Library of Medicine and the National Institute of Health
http://www.nlm.nih.gov/medlineplus/teenagepregnancy.html
This Web site provides information to parents and teens regarding pregnancy, including teen pregnancy articles and newsletters addressing prenatal care and coping with teenage pregnancy; a medical encyclopedia and a medical dictionary; and links to other related sites.

The National Campaign to Prevent Teen Pregnancy
http://www.teenpregnancy.org/
This Web site provides information to teens and parents regarding pregnancy prevention and discussing sexuality.

FATHERING

"To become a father is not difficult, but to be a father is."
—*Unknown*

Fatherhood is hard and very important work. Research has also consistently demonstrated that loving, involved fathers are critically important to their children's health, academic achievement, and general well-being. While the desire to be a father may be inborn, what a responsible father does is learned, and when fathers are absent, children suffer.

Fatherlessness is directly linked to poverty, high school dropout rates, crime, adolescent drug use, and teenage pregnancy. Today, these problems have become too common, with one generation experiencing and then passing on a legacy of fatherlessness. But whether the father is in or out of the home, *every child needs a father he or she can count on*—and mothers often need a partner in parenting. This widespread generational father absence requires that many fathers be trained in what a responsible father does.

The following are some programs to help fathers with the difficult tasks of fatherhood:

Fathers Too: Willing to Serve is a Family, School, and Community Partnerships (FSCP) father involvement initiative. Supported by the Lilly Endowment and the Indiana State Teachers Association, Fathers Too has provided technical assistance and resources to 21 fathers programs since 1997 with the objective of helping men become involved in school safety planning and intervention. While father involvement is beneficial for all youth, low-performing or Title I schools and educationally/economically disadvantaged families particularly reap the benefits of this program. The majority of the program's efforts are concentrated in urban areas, but Fathers Too is an important initiative no matter the location because it focuses not only on the biological father but also on any man who wishes to have a positive impact on a child's life. The program is easily modified to meet the individual needs of schools.

In the Security Dads division, which has been nationally recognized, men serve as mentors and role models for *all* children. According to Dr. Jacqueline Greenwood, principal of Arlington High School, the involvement of fathers has correlated with a decrease in negative student behaviors. Thus, the school has become a safer learning environment. For Fathers Too and its subsidiaries, FSCP provides leadership training, including time management, volunteer recruitment, communication skills, and conflict management. FSCP has also trained two Fathers Too consultants to provide technical assistance to volunteers. The desired outcome is a change in the climate of schools and communities to encourage better grades and improved attendance, more positive behaviors, and a safer environment for families.

For more information about Fathers Too: Willing to Serve, contact program co-founder and FSCP Associate Director Linda Wallace, lwallace@fscp.org, **The Partnerships Center**, 4755 Kingsway Drive, Suite 100, Indianapolis, IN 46205, (317) 205-2595, (866) 391-1039 (toll free).

Fathers and Families Resource/Research Center
2835 N. Illinois Street
Indianapolis, IN
(317) 921-5935
http://www.fatherresource.org
This center provides young fathers with the resources to become responsible and involved parents, wage earners, and providers of support to their children. A secondary objective aims to assist both parents in developing necessary skills and behaviors to care for their children. Programs include fatherhood development classes, Mom's Club, Wash Day reading program, employment preparation, job referrals, co-parenting sessions, anger management, parenting classes, paternity/genetic testing, legal assistance, GED preparation, and financial aid information. It is free.

Fathers in Training
Family Development Services
3637 N. Meridian
Indianapolis, IN
(317) 803-3850
This program offers assistance to Early Head Start and Head Start fathers in facing issues that hinder them from being good fathers by increasing and encouraging involvement in the earliest stages of the child's life. A Gathering of Men is a weekly group that offers men the chance to express themselves and be supported by other fathers. A Gathering of Men and Women focuses on promoting responsible fatherhood and realizing that parenting is a team effort. Child care and dinner are provided for participants.

Raphael Family Life Center: Father Support Program
401 E. 34th Street
Indianapolis, IN
(317) 926-1507
This program offers a 6- to 8-week parenting class for fathers. Topics include paternity, co-parenting, decision-making skills, financial issues, child support issues, and being a positive role model.

Fatherhood Educational Materials

The following materials describe additional programs that promote involvement of fathers in their children's lives. This is not an all-inclusive list, and inclusion on this list is not an endorsement. Curricula should be thoroughly researched before being purchased or used.

The Purdue University Cooperative Extension Service's Human Development Extension has developed two curricula for parents:

- It's My Child, Too! provides parenting training for young fathers who may be having difficulty moving into the role of parenthood. The curriculum was piloted in 1995–1996 with young fathers, about half of whom were temporarily incarcerated. The participants reported increased understanding of the role of fathers in children's lives, ways to interact with children, appropriate approaches to child discipline, effective ways to cope with stress, appropriate communication with their child's mother, and responsibilities of fatherhood.
- Parenting Piece-by-Piece helps parents learn to manage stress, communicate better with their children, use effective discipline, and access community resources for their families. Local training and support is available.

For more information, visit http://www.cfs.purdue.edu/extension/html/hd_home.htm.

The **Fatherhood Workshop Kit**, from **Fatherhood USA**, includes a two-part documentary, *Dedicated, Not Deadbeat* and *Juggling Family and Work*, four video modules, a 24-page facilitator's guide, and a "Fatherhood Tips" handout. It is designed for community-based organizations that want to be more effective in supporting the involvement of fathers in the lives of their children. For more information, see the Fatherhood Project publications order page at http://www.igc.org/fatherhood.

The **National Center for Fathering** offers three kinds of training: online training for interactive training over the Internet; "Train the Trainer" for men interested in training other dads; and "Fathering Training," which includes a variety of training sessions and is led by the National Center for Fathering staff. For more information, visit their Web site at http://www.fathers.com/training.

The **Center for Successful Fathering Inc.** offers the "Accepting the Challenges of Fatherhood" curriculum, which includes a video series. For more information, call the Center at (800) 537-0853 or (512) 335-8106, or e-mail them at rklinger@fathering.org.

There are also new Web sites that focus on fatherhood:

AllProDad.com
Indianapolis Colts coach Tony Dungy is the national spokesman for the All Pro Dad Campaign, the ultimate resource for men who want to become better fathers. This program offers practical fathering assistance updated daily and available 24 hours a day, 365 days a year. The All Pro Dad Web site's premier offering is a free daily e-mail service called "Play of the Day." This service provides dads with hard-hitting information, advice, and inspiration to make them better husbands and fathers. The All Pro Dad program is owned and operated by Family First, 609 West DeLeon Street, Tampa, FL 33606, (813) 222-8300, (800) 956-8300.
http://www.familyfirst.net

Fathers.com
Fathers.com is the premier online resource for everyday dads. Created by the National Center for Fathering, fathers.com provides research-based training, practical tips, and resources to help men be the involved fathers, grandfathers, and father figures their children need.

The National Center for Fathering
P.O. Box 413888
Kansas City, MO 64141
Toll free: (800) 593-DADS
(913) 384-4661
Fax: (913) 384-4665
E-mail: dads@fathers.com

http://www.brandnewdad.com
Especially for new fathers, this is a comprehensive site offering an online community, resource center, and search engine for new and expectant dads.

Below is a list of other sites that cover a broad spectrum of fatherhood-related issues.

American Coalition for Fathers and Children
(800) 978-3237
http://www.acfc.org

At-Home Dad
(508) 685-7931
AtHomeDad@aol.com

Institute for Responsible Fatherhood and Family Revitalization
(202) 293-4420
http://www.responsiblefatherhood.org

National Fatherhood Initiative
(717) 581-8860
http://www.fatherhood.org

National Fathers' Network
(206) 747-4004
http://www.fathersnetwork.org

HOUSING

A safe, stable home is something that most of us take for granted, and appropriate housing is essential for children and adults to reach their full potential. If you are worried about where you are going to sleep tonight, it is very difficult to concentrate on learning or completing a task.

Homeless children are a fast-growing segment of the population, as their numbers have increased 10 percent between 1997 and 2000 to 930,232. Two-thirds are in the age range from pre-K through grade 6. Approximately 87 percent of school-age homeless children and youth are enrolled in school, although only about 77 percent attend school regularly, and only 15 percent of homeless children are in preschool programs, according to the *Report to Congress: Fiscal Year 2000, Education for Homeless Children and Youth Program.*[42]

In reauthorizing the ESEA, Congress amended the Homeless Assistance Act to address the special needs of homeless children and youth. The new **McKinney-Vento** legislation (42 U.S.C. 11431 et seq.) expands and further improves the educational opportunities of homeless children and youth by emphasizing immediate enrollment, transportation, and outreach to youth.

Subtitle VII-B of the McKinney Act (1994 reauthorization) stipulates that:

- *All homeless children and youth have a right to the same free and appropriate public education as other children and youth, including a public preschool education.*
- *States must review and revise residency laws and "other laws, regulations, practices, or policies that may act as a barrier to the enrollment, attendance, or success in school of homeless children and homeless youth."*
- *Students must not be separated from the mainstream school environment because of their homelessness.*
- *Homeless students should have access to educational services to enable them to meet the same challenging student performance standards to which all students are held.*

The Indiana Department of Education (IDOE) has responded to the needs of homeless children. The IDOE Stewart B. McKinney program is part of a federal law called the Improving America's School Act (1994). The initiative supports school corporation programs that facilitate the attendance and success in school of homeless preschoolers, children, and youth. There

[42]*Education for Homeless Children and Youth Program.* http://www.ed.gov/offices/OUS/PES/ed_for_disadvantaged.html#succeed. 1/04/05.

were 16 Stewart B. McKinney project sites during the 2001–2002 school year.[43]

The IDOE has also developed the *Education of Homeless Children and Youth (EHCY) Self-Assessment Guide for Schools* with the philosophy that schools can make a difference by providing a stabilizing environment, a haven from the chaos of homelessness, and a quality educational experience to empower students in homeless situations to break the cycles of poverty, dependency, and homelessness. Schools can be a critical link between the community and children without homes and their families.[44]

School to provide homeless liaisons

The McKinney-Vento Act also calls on schools to put homeless liaisons in schools to act as a contact person for homeless families. The liaisons are to be provided with information to help them assist homeless children and youth with enrolling and successfully attending school. School liaisons are an integral link to academic and future economic success for children and youth experiencing the difficult conditions of homelessness.

Resources for families who are homeless or renting and wanting to buy a home:

HELPLINE 2-1-1
(317) 926-4357 or dial 2-1-1

HELPLINE 2-1-1 provides information about and referral to social service resources in central Indiana. Resources include food pantries, emergency shelters, legal services, support groups, financial counseling, government services, educational services, addiction programs, medical services, employment programs, and much more. HELPLINE 2-1-1 services are confidential and provided at no charge. HELPLINE 2-1-1 is answered live 24 hours a day, 7 days a week, with expert assistance available 8 a.m. to 8 p.m. and direct connection to shelters and crisis services from 8 p.m. to 8 a.m. Spanish-speaking specialists are generally available Monday through Friday, 9 a.m. to 5 p.m.

---

[43]Descriptions of the programs in Indiana can be found at http://www.doe.state.in.us/alted/currentmckinneyprograms.html.

[44]To review this guide, see http://www.doe.state.in.us/alted/homelessassesmentlinkpg.html.

Indiana Coalition on Housing and Homeless Issues Inc. (ICHHI)
324 West Morris Street, Suite 202
Indianapolis, IN 46225
(317) 636-8819
Fax: 317-636-8383
E-mail: info@ichhi.org
http://www.ichhi.org
The Indiana Coalition on Housing and Homeless Issues (ICHHI) is a statewide association dedicated to the right of all Indiana citizens to safe, decent, and affordable housing and necessary supportive services.

Comprando Casa (Hispanic Education Center)
580 E. Stevens Street
Indianapolis, IN 46203
(317) 634-5022
(317) 465-0039
This program offers Hispanics information, guidance, and assistance with purchasing their first home. Orientation is required to assess whether a family is eligible for the program, which assists families in becoming eligible if not currently eligible and obtaining a mortgage loan and a real estate agent. This service is provided during and after the buying process and is free.

Family Development for Home Ownership
615 N. Alabama Street, Suite 320
Indianapolis, IN 46204
(317) 926-4739
http://www.family-service-inc.org
This program assists families with housing options. It provides housing-, credit-, and debt-management counseling to families or individuals working toward home ownership.

Indianapolis Neighborhood Housing Partnership
3550 N. Washington Boulvard
Indianapolis, IN 46205
(317) 925-1400
http://www.inhp.org
This program matches homebuyers and homeowners with available resources for mortgage loans and financing home repairs. INHP can provide credit-worthy customers with low-interest loans for repairs, down payments, and other costs that go with buying a home. Pre- and post-purchase counseling is available at no charge to help families improve their credit and work on other issues in their pursuit of home ownership or home repairs. It also offers free classes to potential homebuyers that include an overview of each

step in the buying process, including information about the steps to obtain a mortgage, money management/credit issues, home inspection, homeowner's insurance, shopping for a home, closing information, and the benefits of home ownership. It is based on sliding-scale fees.

Habitat for Humanity of Greater Indianapolis
(317) 921-2121
http://www.indyhabitat.org
This program builds and sells homes for very low income persons. Eligible clients contribute 175 hours of labor toward construction of a dwelling that they may then purchase through a no-interest loan. The waiting period is six months. It serves Hancock, Johnson, and Marion Counties and can make referrals to statewide programs.

U.S. Department of Housing and Urban Development (HUD)
451 7th Street S.W.
Washington, DC 20410
(202) 708-1112
TTY: (202) 708-1455

Subsidized Housing
151 N. Delaware, Suite 1200
Indianapolis, IN 46204
(317) 226-6303
http://www.hud.gov
The national Web site has a link to Indiana resources for housing, homelessness, food and clothing, free health care, and jobs and training.

EMPLOYMENT

Parents worry. It's just what they do. However, *what* parents worry about depends on their individual circumstances and situations. This book encourages parents to be concerned and, yes, to worry about their children's education. Do my children have a good teacher? Does their class work meet the state's standards? Are they taking the right classes to help them get into college? These are all important questions for parents to ask, but they probably will not get answered, or even asked, if parents are worried about more immediate concerns such as shelter, food, and clothing. Shelter, food, and clothing are basic needs not only for children but adults as well, and they all require money. And in order to have money, a parent must have a job that pays enough to support a family. If you need help finding a job, or a better job, there are services available at no cost to help.

U.S. Department of Labor
Frances Perkins Building
200 Constitution Avenue, N.W.
Washington, DC 20210
(866) 4-USA-DOL
TTY: (877) 889-5627
http://www.dol.gov
The mission of the **21st Century Workforce Office** is to ensure that all American workers have as fulfilling and financially rewarding a career as they aspire to have and to make sure that no worker gets left behind in the limitless potential of the dynamic, global economy of this new millennium. The department provides a wealth of resources for job seekers and anyone looking for career information.

Indiana Department of Labor
State Office Building
402 W. Washington Street, Room W195
Indianapolis, IN 46204-2751
http://www.in.gov/labor/

Information Regarding Employment Programs

Fathers and Families Resource and Research Center
2835 N. Illinois Street
Indianapolis, IN
(317) 921-5935
http://www.fatherresource.org
This service provides young fathers with resources to become responsible and involved parents, wage earners, and providers of support to their children. A

secondary objective aims to assist both parents in developing necessary skills to care for their children. Programs include fatherhood development classes, Mom's Club, Wash Day reading program, employment preparation, job referrals, co-parenting sessions, anger management, parenting classes, paternity/genetic testing, legal assistance, GED preparation, and financial aid information. It is free.

Goodwill Industries
Services at various locations throughout Indiana
(317) 524-4313
http://www.goodwill-indy.org
This program offers supported employment for people with disabilities, case management, individual assessment, career exploration, job placement, self-esteem building, computer training, and goal setting. It also provides help with child care and transportation costs and can work with ex-offenders.

Indianapolis Urban League
777 Indiana Avenue
Indianapolis, IN
(317) 693-7603
http://www.indplsul.org
This program offers job guidance and career development workshops and counsels on résumé writing, application process, and interviewing skills. It maintains client and employer job bank and refers clients to job openings and is free.

Indypendence
222 E. Ohio Street, Suite 300
Indianapolis, IN
(317) 524-6760
This program helps young women obtain their GED or high school diploma. It offers vocational training in retail sales, business technology, clerical, certified nursing assistant (CNA), and hotel hospitality for six to 24 months. The program is available to females ages 16 to 24, with priority given to young mothers. It provides assistance with transportation, meals, books/supplies, and basic medical care and also provides a modest living and clothing allowance and assists with job placement.
For programs nationwide, call (800) 733-5627 (JOBS).

Ivy Tech State College
1 W. 26th Street
Indianapolis, IN
(317) 921-4795
http://www.ivytech.edu
This college offers vocational and career interest testing and guidance to adults 18 and older. It is free, and programs are offered statewide.

Training Inc.
333 N. Pennsylvania
Indianapolis, IN
(317) 264-6740
http://www.traininginc.org
This program provides an assessment program to develop a career plan, identify current skills, and determine what skills are needed. Scholarships are available, and this program is free. It is available to adults 18 or older who are on TANF or food stamps or are economically disadvantaged.

WIA (Workforce Investment Act)
(317) 624-2400
This program offers job placement for displaced workers and low-income and disabled adults 16 and older. It provides job searches, job matching, skill assessment, career counseling, and résumé assistance. It is free and serves Marion, Hamilton, Hendricks, Johnson, and Morgan Counties.

WorkOne Express
(317) 684-7601
This program offers job placement for displaced workers and low-income and disabled individuals 14 and older. It provides job searches, job matching, skill assessment, career counseling, and résumé assistance. It is free and serves Shelby, Hancock, Boone, and Marion Counties.

EMERGENCY SERVICES

"Emergency" is defined as a serious situation or occurrence that happens *unexpectedly* and demands *immediate* action. Parents do not—and cannot—plan emergencies, and no matter how great they are as parents, emergencies can still happen. Therefore, it is in a family's best interest to be prepared should an emergency arise.

Helpful telephone numbers for many different emergencies that may occur in your family follow:

911: This number can be used for all emergencies including fires, crimes, and medical emergencies. It can be dialed from all telephones including cell phones.

Medical Emergencies:
Make sure that the telephone numbers of all family doctors are posted near the phone and accessible to all members of the family. It is also helpful to keep a list of family members' allergies handy.

Fire Prevention:
It is important to have evacuation routes planned and practiced with your children. Also, it is necessary to have at least one *working* smoke detector and one fire extinguisher on every level of your home. If you are in need of smoke detectors, you may obtain one from your local fire department. For more information, call (317) 327-6006.

Poison Control: (800) 222-1222
(800) 222-1222 is the telephone number for every poison center in the United States. Call this number 24 hours a day, 7 days a week, to talk to a poison expert. By telling the poison control employee what and how much your child ingested, he or she can inform you whether hospital assistance is necessary or whether it can be managed in the home.

Child Abuse: (800) 800-5556
This is the statewide telephone number to report child abuse. If you know or suspect a child is being abused, please call this number! Reports can be made anonymously. Reporting saves lives!

Respite Services: Family Support Center (317) 634-5050
There are times when even the best parents become stressed and frustrated. Hopefully, you have support systems in your life that you can rely on in times like these to talk, to listen, or to help you with your children. However, if you don't have these supports, the Family Support Center is available. The Family Support Center is a temporary emergency shelter for children ages

0 to 17 to provide relief for parents who are under stress, homeless, or at risk for abuse and/or neglect. Parents may voluntarily place their children at the Family Support Center for one or more days. They also provide crisis intervention, limited aftercare, and a referral to community resource.

Youth Emergency Services: (317) 917-7700
Youth Emergency Services (YES) is a 24-hour-a-day, 7-days-a-week service that offers crisis intervention to children and families at risk. YES accepts self-referrals for safety plans and crisis sessions as well as referrals to community resources.

Crisis Lines:
(317) 926-HELP
(317) 251-7575

These crisis lines offer crisis assistance and referrals 24 hours a day, 7 days a week.

RUNAWAYS

According to Indiana law, a runaway is "**a child [who] ... leaves home without reasonable cause and without permission of the parent, guardian, or custodian who requests the child's return**" (Indiana Code IC 31-37-2-2). Your child does not have to be gone for a specified period of time before you report him or her as a runaway. He or she can be gone for only five minutes! It is extremely important that as a parent/guardian, you report your child as a runaway if he or she is gone without your permission or if you are unaware of his or her whereabouts, because you are legally responsible for your child and any actions he or she may commit!

Each community in Indiana may handle runaways differently. To find out how to handle a runaway in your area, contact the local police station. As an example of how these situations are handled, we have illustrated the procedures used in Marion County as a guide.

In Marion County, if your child runs away, **you as the parent/guardian are responsible** for doing the following:

1. **File a missing persons report** with the police department that patrols your area. (See contact numbers and additional information below.)
2. If your child returns home after the report has been filed, call the police department that patrols your area.
3. Your child will be taken (by law enforcement) to the **Back to Home** Center located at 4144 N. Keystone Avenue, Indianapolis, IN 46205, (317) 917-7700, where a Back to Home Runaway Crisis Counselor will meet your child and the transporting officer.
4. During the intake, it will be determined whether your child is on probation and, if so, violating the probation agreement and therefore should be transported to juvenile detention.
5. The next step of the intake includes a crisis counselor immediately conducting an assessment of your child to insure that he or she is safe, not under the influence of drugs and/or alcohol, and to determine his or her reasons for running away from home.
6. Next, as parent/guardian, you will be contacted to pick up your child and participate in a meeting with the runaway crisis counselor. This request is so you can complete the assessment process and contribute your ideas and reasons for the runaway behavior.
7. The runaway crisis counselor will work with you to discover your family's strengths and community supports that can be utilized to reduce or prevent further runaway behavior. This family meeting will result in a safety plan that will list what all members of the family will do to help solve this issue. This session could include referrals to outside agencies for other services.

8. A runaway crisis counselor will contact you within 72 hours to check on you and your child. The counselor can offer services over the phone or schedule another family meeting.
9. Back to Home also offers ongoing case management services to link families to community-based services and provide additional support.

Back to Home is available 24 hours a day, 7 days a week, for crisis intervention. Call (317) 917-7700.

PART V

Resource List

Organizations

Alliance for School Choice, http://www.allianceforschoolchoice.org
American Council on Education, http://www.acenet.edu
Center on School, Family, and Community Partnerships,
  http://www.csos.jhu.edu/p2000/center.htm
Communities in Schools, http://www.cisnet.org/index.html
Exceptional Parent Magazine, http://www.eparent.com
Families and Schools Together, http://www.wcer.wisc.edu/fast/
Family Support America, http://www.familysupportamerica.org/content/home.htm
Foundations Inc., http://www.foundations-inc.org/
GED on TV, http://www.gedontv.org
Get Ready to Read, http://www.getreadytoread.org
Goodwill Industries of Central Indiana,
  http://www.goodwill-indy.org/education.htm
Greater Educational Opportunities Foundation, http://www.geofoundation.org/
Indiana Coalition against Domestic Violence, http://www.violenceresource.org
Indiana Commission for Higher Education, http://www.che.state.in.us/
Indiana Department of Education, http://www.doe.state.in.us/
Indiana Family and Social Services Administration, http://www.in.gov/fssa/
Indiana Literacy Foundation, http://www.indianaliteracy.org/
Institute for Educational Leadership, http://www.iel.org/
Institute for Responsive Education, http://www.resp-ed.org/
Job Corps, http://jobcorps.doleta.gov/centers/in.cfm
National Association of Partners in Education, http://www.napehq.org/
National Center for Community Education, http://www.nccenet.org/
National Coalition for Parent Involvement in Education (NCPIE), http://www.ncpie.org/
National Community Education Association (NCEA), http://www.ncea.com/
National Network of Partnership Schools, http://www.csos.jhu.edu/p2000/
National Parent Information Network (NPIN), http://www.npin.org/
National Parent Teacher Association, http://www.pta.org/index.stm
National Right to Read Foundation, http://www.nrrf.org/
No Child Left Behind: A Parents Guide,
  http://www.ed.gov/parents/academic/involve/nclbguide/parentsguide.html
Office of Vocational and Adult Education, http://www.ed.gov
Parents as Teachers National Center, http://www.patnc.org/
Parents for Public Schools, http://www.parents4publicschools.com/
Partnership for Family Involvement in Education, http://www.pfie.ed.gov/

Proactive Parent, http://www.proactiveparent.com
Protective Order Pro Bono Project, http://www.popbp.org
Reading Is Fundamental, http://www.rif.org
Regional Educational Laboratory Network, http://www.relnetwork.org/
Starfish Initiative, http://www.starfishinitiative.org
The Education Trust, http://www2.edtrust.org/edtrust
The Teen Worker, http://www.in.gov/labor/childlabor/
U.S. Department of Education, http://www.ed.gov/
U.S. Department of Education listing of Parent Resource Centers (lists centers for all states), http://www.ed.gov/Programs/bastmp/PRC.htm
Youth as Resources of Central Indiana, http://www.uwci.org/yar/

Tools

Checklist of How to Increase Parent Involvement, http://www.maec.org/tadocs/parent.html
Developing Family/School Partnerships: Guidelines for Schools and School Districts, http://www.coopext.colostate.edu/PIP/parenteducator/pejan99.pdf
Educational Choice Charitable Trust, http://choicetrust.org
Family Guide to Public Schools in Indianapolis, http://imaps.indygov.org/schools, available in English or Spanish
Federal Student Aid for Higher Education, http://www.fafsa.ed.gov/index.htm
Get Ready to Read! http://www.getreadytoread.org/
GreatSchools.net, http://www.greatschools.net/
Indiana's Academic Standards and Resources, http://www.indianastandardsresources.org/
Indiana Accountability System for Academic Programs, http://www.doe.state.in.us/asap/welcome.html
Indiana Non-Public Education Association, http://www.inpea.org
ISTEP+ Info Center, http://www.doe.state.in.us/istep/
Learn More Resource Center, http://www.learnmoreindiana.org
My Career Education, Indiana Schools and Colleges, http://www.my-career-education.com/indiana.htm
National Standards for Parent/Family Involvement Programs, http://www.pta.org/programs/invstand.htm
Parent Involvement Survey, http://www.maec.org/frameset.php
ProactiveParent.com, http://www.proactiveparent.com/
School and Family Involvement Surveys, http://www.ncrel.org/cscd/sfi/
The Possibility Network, http://www.indianalearn.com/pla/lotech.jsp?&flash_enabled=true&

Charter Schools

Charter School Service Center, http://www.geofoundation.org
Indiana Charter Schools, http://www.doe.state.in.us/charterschools
Indiana Charter School Law and Resources, http://www.charterschoollaw.com
Mayor of Indianapolis, http://www.indygov.org/mayor/charter
Ball State University, http://www.bsu.edu/teachers/charter

Non-Public Schools

American Association of Christian Schools, http://www.aacs.org
Association of Christian Schools International, http://www.acsi.org
Boarding Schools, http://www.schools.com
Catholic Schools, http://www.archindy.org
Catholic Boarding Schools, http://www.cbsa.org
Christian Schools, http://www.christianschoolsusa.com
Independent Schools, http://www.isacs.org
Indiana Non-Public Education Association, http://www.inpea.org
Lutheran Schools, http://www.indylutheranschools.org
Montessori Schools, http://www.amshq.org
Private School Locator, http://www.nces.ed.gov
Seventh Day Adventist Schools, http://www.nadeducation.adventist.org

Home Schooling

Indiana Association of Home Educators, http://www.inhomeeducators.org
Indiana Foundation for Home Schooling, http://www.IFHSonline.org
Indiana Department of Education, http://doe.state.in.us/sservices/hse.htm.
Homeschooling Your Children, http://educate.barnesandnoble.com.
Home School Legal Defense Association, http://www.hslda.org
National Black Home Educators Resource Association, nbhera@Internet8.net
National Challenged Homeschoolers Associated Network, http://www.nathhan.com
National Home Education Network, http://www.nhen.org

Child Care

All-American Nanny Ltd., nanny@pinn.net
Child Care Aware, http://www.childcareaware.org
Child Care Finder, http://www.childcarefinder.in.gov
Indiana Association for Child Care Resource and Referral, http://www.iaccrr.org
National Association for the Education of Young Children, http://naeyc.org/

Special Needs

Exceptional Parent Magazine, http://www.eparent.com
IDEA regulations Section 300.347, http://www.access.gpo.gov/su_docs/fedreg/a990312c.html
National Information Center for Children and Youth with Disabilities, http://www.nichcy.org
PACER Center, http://www.pacer.org
Wrightslaw Yellow Pages for Kids with Disabilities, http://www.yellowpagesforkids.com/

Tutoring

Homework Hotline, http://www.askrose.org
Indiana Reading Corps, http://www.indianacampuscompact.org
Online Tutoring in Indiana, http://www.anysubject.com/us/Indiana.htm
Tutor.com, http://www.tutor.com/
Young Child Education: Games and Online Tutoring, http://www.young-child-education.org/

Military

U.S. Army, http://www.goarmy.com
U.S. Coast Guard, http://www.gocoastguard.com
U.S. Marines, http://www.marines.com
U.S. National Guard, http://www.1800goguard.com
U.S. Navy, http://www.navy.com

College

21st Century Scholars Statewide, http://www.scholars.indiana.edu
College Board, http://www.collegeboard.com
FastWeb, http://www.fastweb.monster.com
Free Scholarships, http://www.freescholarshipguide.com
Get College Funds, http://www.getcollegefunds.org
GoCollege, http://www.gocollege.com
Indiana College Answers, http://www.indiana.wiredscholar.com
Making It Count, http://www.makingcollegecount.com/
The Princeton Review, College Admissions Testing, http://www.princetonreview.com/college/testprep/
Smart Student Guide to Financial Aid, http://www.smart1.fiinaid.org
State Student Assistance Commission of Indiana, http://www.ai.org/ssaci/programs/index.html

PART VI

Glossary

ACCOUNTABILITY
Policies developed to hold schools and school systems responsible for the academic results of their students.

ACHIEVEMENT GAP
The difference in school achievement among different groups of students, such as racial/ethnic groups, income levels, etc.

ACT
The ACT is a standardized college admissions test used to determine eligibility for admission to colleges and universities.

ADHD (ATTENTION-DEFICIT/HYPERACTIVITY DISORDER)
A group of disorders causing difficulty controlling behavior, paying attention, and/or remaining still.

AYP (ADEQUATE YEARLY PROGRESS)
A signaling system to tell whether schools are on track to teach all students what they need to know in each school year.

CONTENT STANDARDS
Statements of what students from kindergarten through twelfth grade should know and be able to do in the core content areas: for example, English/language arts, mathematics, science, and social studies.

CORE 40 DIPLOMA
A diploma earned by successfully completing 40 credits in required and optional approved secondary school courses.

CURRICULUM
The subject material that teachers cover with students in class.

DATA
Facts or figures from which conclusions can be made; information.

DISAGGREGATE
To breakdown information by different groups, either by race, ethnicity, income levels, gender, etc.

GED (GENERAL EDUCATION DIPLOMA)
A earned when 17 years old or older in place of a high school diploma.

GQE (GRADUATE QUALIFYING EXAMINATION)
A continuation of the ISTEP+ program that students must pass to graduate from high school in Indiana.

IDOE
The Indiana Department of Education.

IN NEED OF IMPROVEMENT
The term established the No Child Left Behind legislation used to describe Title I schools failing to make adequate yearly progress in improving student achievement as defined by the state for two consecutive years or longer.

ISTEP+ (INDIANA STATEWIDE TESTING FOR EDUCATIONAL PROGRESS-PLUS)
A criterion-referenced assessment to measure student academic progress in Indiana.

LEA (LOCAL EDUCATIONAL AGENCY)
A school district.

LEP (LIMITED ENGLISH PROFICIENCY)
An individual whose primary/native language is not English.

NCLB (NO CHILD LEFT BEHIND)
The most significant federal education initiative signed by President Bush in 2001. The law provides opportunities for families of students enrolled in schools that are "in need of improvement," including choosing a higher-performing public school or free tutoring.

OPPORTUNITY GAP
Differences in resources available to different schools: for example, buildings, money, teachers, and other resources such as those in the community and at home, such as neighborhood libraries, personal computers, and home reference materials.

PROFESSIONAL DEVELOPMENT
The ongoing training of teachers.

PROFICIENCY
This means a student is able to do something he or she is supposed to do at that age and grade level, based on content standards.

SAT (SCHOLASTIC ASSESSMENT TEST)
A standardized college admissions test used to determine eligibility for admission to colleges and universities.

SUPPLEMENTAL SERVICES
Services provided outside the regular school day to help students reach proficiency. These are paid for with federal Title I funds.

TITLE I
The first section of the Elementary and Secondary Elementary Act. Refers to programs aimed at America's most disadvantaged students. Provides assistance to improve the education of children in high-poverty schools, enabling those children to meet state academic content and performance standards.

TITLE I SCHOOL
If the number of low-income students is above 40 percent, schools may use Title I funds to create school-wide programs to improve achievement, thereby serving all children in the school.

PART VII

Bibliography

11 Tips To Help Parents Create Safer Schools. KSA Plus Communications http://www.ksaplus.com.

A Parent's Guide to School Involvement. National Education Association. October 22, 2003. http://www.nea.org/parents/schoolinvolve.html.

As a Parent, Here Are 12 Things You Should Know about and Expect from Your Schools ... and Yourself. Parent Leadership Associates. October 22, 2003. http://www.plassociates.org/twelve.html.

Baker, E., Herman, J., and Bain, J. *What Makes a Good School: A Guide for Parents Seeking Excellence in Education.*

Bolick, C. *Voucher Wars.*

Byrk, S., Easton, J. Q., Kerbow, D., Rollow, S., and Bender Sebring, P. *Charting Chicago School Reform: Democratic Localism as a Lever for Change*. Boulder, CO: Westview Press, 1998.

"Charter Schools." Office of the Mayor, City of Indianapolis. http://www.indygov.org/eGov/Mayor/Education/Charter/home.htm.

"Choosing Better Schools: a Report on Student Transfers under the No Child Left Behind Act." Report of the Citizen's Commission on Civil Rights. May 2004. C. G. Brown, Principal and Investigator.

Cotton, K., and Conklin, N. F. *Research on Early Childhood Education*, School Improvement Research Series, Northwest Regional Educational Laboratory. http://www.nwrel.org/scpd/sirs/3/topsyn3.html.

Crabtree, R. K., Esq. *The Paper Chase: Managing Your Child's Documents under the IDEA*. http://www.fetaweb.com/03/paperchase.crabtree.htm.

Cromwell, S. "A Recent U.S. Department of Education Report Looks at the Differences and Similarities of Public and Private Schools." Education World (1997).

Education for Homeless Children and Youth Program. http://www.ed.gov/offices/OUS/PES/ed_for_disadvantaged.html#succeed.

"GED Opens Doors for Hoosiers." Indiana Department of Education.

Getting Involved in Your Child's Education. National Education Association. October 22, 2003. http://www.nea.org/parents/.

Greene, J. P., Ph.D., and Forster, G., Ph.D. *Public High School Graduation and College Readiness Rates in the United States.*

How Do I Know If My Child's Teacher Is Qualified? October 30, 2003. http://www.eric.ed.gov/.

"How to Advocate for Your Child." *Parent Power Newsletter*. The Center for Education Reform, Washington, D.C. August 2001.

How to Tell If Your Child May Be in Trouble with Alcohol. December 1, 2004. The National Council on Alcoholism and Drug Dependence Inc. http://www.ncadd.org/facts/parent2.html.

Howell, W. G., and Peterson, P. E. *The Education Gap.*
"Improving Your Schools: A Parent and Community Guide to No Child Left Behind." The Education Trust. Fall 2003.
Indiana Charter School Law. Indiana Department of Education. November 7, 2004. http://www.doe.state.in.us/charterschools/welcome.html.
Indiana State Department of Health. *Births and Age-Specific Rates by Race and Age of Mother: Indiana.* 1999.
"Indiana Schools up to Challenge; 76 percent Make Adequate Yearly Progress." Indiana Department of Education. http://www.doe.state.in.us/reed/newsr04/July2004/ayp2003table-release.html.
"Indiana Policy under the Unsafe School Choice Option, No Child Left Behind Act of 2001." Adopted April 30, 2003.
"Individualized Education Program (IEP): Some Suggestions to Consider." *Exceptional Parent* Magazine. http://www.eparent.com/education/idea04_05.htm.
Kugler, E. "*Finding a 'Good School.'*" October 22, 2003. http://www.pta.org/parentinvolvement/parenttalk/goodschool.asp.
Malignant Neglect: Substance Abuse and America's Schools. National Center on Addiction and Substance Abuse at Columbia University, NY. September 2001.
http://www.casacolumbia.org/pdshopprov/files/80624.pdf.
Mapp, K., and Henderson, A. *A New Wave of Evidence: The Impact of School, Family and Community Connections on Student Achievement.* Southeast Educational Developmental Laboratory. 2002. http://www.sedl.org/connections/resources/evidence.pdf.
Minter Hoxby, C. Harvard University and Stanford University's Hoover Institute Study.
Minter Hoxby, C. Center for Education Reform. Harvard University and Stanford University's Hoover Institute.
Neal, D. *Resources and Educational Outcomes among Black Children.*
Patten, P. "The Fourth 'R': Teacher-Child Relationships Are Central to Quality." *Parent News.* March–April 2001.
Rosenthal, Lisa. *An Apple a Day Can't Keep the Junk Food away from the School Cafeteria.* http://www.GreatSchools.net.
School Quality. National Education Association. October 30, 2003. http://www.nea.org/schoolquality/.
Snow, C. E., Burns, M. S., and Griffin, P. *Starting out Right.* Committee on the Prevention of Reading Difficulties in Young Children. National Academy of Sciences, Washington, D.C. 1998
Teen Pregnancy Statistics and Prevention. http://www.familyfirstaid.org/teen-pregnancy.html.
Things Parents Can Do to Help Students Succeed. Learn More Resource Center Web site. http://www.learnmoreindiana.org/@parents/parents_68/support_learning/quick_tips.xml.
Thernstrom, A., and Thernstrom, S. *No Excuses.*
Tools for Student Success. U.S. Department of Education. http://www.ed.gov/parents/academic/help/tools-for-success/index.html.
"Top Ten Questions to Ask When Choosing Your Child's School." 1996. *Parent News. 2.3:* 16.
What the Research Says. National Education Association. October 22, 2003. http://www.nea.org/parents/research-parents.html.